THE

RUNNER'S WORLD
VEGETARIAN
COOKBOOK

150 Delicious and Nutritious Meatless Recipes
to Fuel Your Every Step

Heather Mayer Irvine

RODALE

New York

For my Bobie, who always told me I could do anything
I wanted to do and be anything I wanted to be

Live happy. Be healthy. Get inspired.

Mention of specific companies,
organizations, or authorities in this
book does not imply endorsement by
the author or publisher, nor does
mention of specific companies,
organizations, or authorities imply
that they endorse this book, its
author, or the publisher. Internet
addresses and phone numbers given
in this book were accurate at the
time it went to press.

Published in the United States by
Rodale Books, an imprint of the
Crown Publishing Group, a division
of Penguin Random House LLC,
New York.
crownpublishing.com
rodalebooks.com
Runner's World® is a registered
trademark of Hearst Magazines, Inc.

RODALE and the Plant colophon are
registered trademarks of
Penguin Random House LLC.

Many of the recipes in this work have
been previously published, some in
different form.

Library of Congress Cataloging-in-
Publication Data is available upon
request.

ISBN 978-1-63565-061-7
Ebook ISBN 978-1-63565-062-4

Printed in China

Book design by Yeon Kim
Book photographs by Mitch Mandel
Food styling by Adrienne Anderson
Prop styling by Paola Andrea

10 9 8 7 6 5 4 3 2 1
First Edition

 RODALE

Follow us @RodaleBooks on 🐦 f 📌 📷

We inspire health, healing,
happiness, and love in the world.
Starting with you.

CONTENTS

FOREWORD

▶ In today's modern world of overwhelming food options and constantly evolving nutritional advice, one piece of age-old wisdom still rings true: Eat more plants. Science also agrees that eating more whole, plant-based foods is the best way to promote health and ward off disease. If a diet promotes health and can prevent—and even reverse—disease, it surely can improve performance and recovery in runners of all levels.

Growing up in northern Minnesota, I spent a lot of time in family gardens, preparing the soil, planting, weeding, and—the best part—harvesting. Pulling a young carrot from the earth, brushing the soil off, and sinking my teeth into the orange crunchiness has been forever etched into my memory. I can taste the flavors just thinking about it. Even though my childhood vegetable ensemble consisted mostly of carrots, potatoes, and sweet corn, eating fresh fruits and vegetables was always a part of my diet. That practice laid the groundwork for understanding the importance of eating fresh, whole plant foods.

I also spent a lot of time in the kitchen, preparing and preserving the food my family harvested. Some of my earliest memories as a child were kneading bread dough with my grandmother and hand-mixing cookie dough with my mother. I would grip the spoon and try to move it through the dense mixture until my mother came to the rescue, supporting my hands and the spoon as she whirled it around the bowl. There was a simple beauty and satisfaction in watching the ingredients transform into a dish. That amazement comes alive whenever I am in the kitchen preparing a meal, and it never gets old.

Later, when I started cross-country skiing and running competitively, I began to see food not only as a connection to the land and kitchen, but as fuel for performance. In my high school and college years I expanded my palate to be more accepting of vegetables because I knew they were important to recovery. I was now making my sandwiches with spinach and eating heaping mounds of steamed broccoli with my meat and potatoes.

I really opened my mind when I decided to transition to a vegetarian diet, and ultimately became fully vegan. Rather than look at my new plant-based diet as one that eliminates all animal foods and could result in deficiencies if not done right, I started to view it as a refreshing way to try new plant foods and be adventurous. Most of these foods I had never heard of, nor tried—think chickpeas, flaxseeds, kale, and quinoa—and I certainly didn't want to. Remember, I was the kid who had a hard time with vegetables except for potatoes, corn, and *raw* carrots—I hated them cooked.

Over the years, I have learned a lot about plant-based nutrition, but more importantly, I've learned how to be comfortable in the kitchen and make tasty, balanced meals with more whole plant foods. While I love to experiment with complex recipes and new ingredients, I still go back to the basics of nutrition I learned decades ago: Eat fresh, whole plants, and prepare them yourself. My mother always believed that cooking shouldn't be complex and that you didn't need to be a great chef to cook delicious food. She used to say, "If you can read, you can cook." I couldn't agree more.

The editors at *Runner's World* and *The Runner's World Vegetarian Cookbook* agree with my mom, too. The pages of the magazine and this cookbook are filled with nutritious, delicious, and easy meals that will power your runs and recovery, no matter your dietary preference.

Eating and preparing food should be looked at as part of a lifestyle and training, much like getting out the door and logging miles or hitting the gym for strength training. When I talk to runners, most tell me they want to be running well into their golden years. That goal is more achievable when you look at diet as a long-term path to total health instead of a quick fix to shed a few pounds.

Whether you are a runner who wants to experiment with a plant-based diet or simply incorporate more whole plant foods into your diet and busy running lifestyle, *The Runner's World Vegetarian Cookbook* will help power your body with plant fuel that is easy and delicious to prepare. Keep eating those plants and get in that kitchen!

SCOTT JUREK
WORLD-RENOWNED ULTRAMARATHON CHAMPION

INTRODUCTION: EAT MORE PLANTS

▶ There's no doubt that more and more runners are going green. Elite runners who nix meat—and even those who cut out animal products altogether—are still coming out on top (one only needs to think of Scott Jurek of ultrarunning and plant-based eating fame to realize this is true).

Eating more veggies and plant foods takes a lesser toll on the environment, forces runners to think outside the pasta-and-meat-sauce box, and invites a whole host of nutrients into the diet that will support any workout and recovery.

But just because you've picked up a vegetarian cookbook doesn't mean you have to forgo your post-marathon burger. Regardless of your food-with-a-face preference, ramping up your plant intake can help you run strong.

In the pages of *Runner's World,* we celebrate runners of all shapes and sizes, abilities, and dietary preferences. At the end of the day, we want you to be inspired to put down our magazine and go for a run, come back and prepare a healthy snack to refuel, and then go on to plan your next run.

Many of these dishes can be prepared in 30 minutes or less. Many are also vegan-friendly, and they are noted as such. If you're trying to lose weight, it's still important to fuel your body with good foods. Follow the "low-calorie" tags, which indicate recipes that are 400 calories or fewer but still have the nutrients you need to run long and hard.

These pages are filled with some of the best veggie recipes developed by *Runner's World,* the Rodale Test Kitchen, and contributors like elite runners Matt Llano, Deena Kastor, Scott Jurek, and Shalane Flanagan and Elyse Kopecky, coauthors of the *New York Times* bestseller *Run Fast. Eat Slow* (Rodale, 2016).

We hope this vegetarian cookbook, the third in the *Runner's World* cookbook series, will encourage you to put a new plant-based item in your shopping cart every week and try your hand at a new dish that doesn't rely on meat for your protein fix. Or if you've already ditched meat, we hope these 150 recipes, all vetted by the Rodale Test Kitchen, will bring something new and exciting to your plate.

Happy running, and of course, happy cooking!

HEATHER MAYER IRVINE
FORMER FOOD AND NUTRITION EDITOR, *RUNNER'S WORLD*

WHAT VEGETARIANS AND VEGANS NEED TO KNOW ABOUT FUELING THEIR RUNS

Runners of all paces and mileage need to feed their bodies quality nutrition in order to boost performance and aid recovery. But non-meat-eaters and plant-based runners have to try a little harder to make sure they're getting enough of certain nutrients most commonly found in animal products, like protein and vitamin B_{12}.

Follow these six tenets and you'll find yourself feeling healthy, running strong, recovering quickly, maintaining a healthy weight, and, of course, enjoying every meal.

1. Eat all the colors.

In the pages of *Runner's World,* we encourage our readers to "eat the rainbow." Choosing produce of all different colors is the best way to get all the nutrients you need.

For example, the orange in vegetables, like carrots and butternut squash, means there are high levels of beta-carotene, which ultimately becomes vitamin A, for immune and eye health. The red in tomatoes comes from lycopene, a powerful antioxidant thought to help ward off cancer and decrease your risk of stroke. Bright colors also indicate the food is rich in antioxidants, which can fight heart disease and Alzheimer's disease.

While taking vitamin supplements can be beneficial in some circumstances, it's important to remember that they're just that—*supplements.* It's best to get your vitamins and minerals from whole foods. Studies suggest that the pigments in produce need to interact with each other in order to maximize the health benefits, meaning a supplement of beta-carotene won't have the same effect as your afternoon snack of baby carrots. Whole foods also offer health benefits that pills can't, like boosting digestive health and making you feel full thanks to their fiber content. And they taste great, too!

Runners should aim for nine servings of fruits and veggies every day. For reference, a serving equals a medium-size piece of fresh fruit, $\frac{1}{3}$ cup of dried fruit, 1 cup of raw veggies, $\frac{1}{2}$ cup of cooked veggies, or 2 cups of salad greens. When you add fruits and veggies to recipes—like stuffed omelets, stir-fries, and everything-but-the-kitchen-sink salads—it's easy to get your recommended servings.

When it comes to fresh versus frozen produce, there isn't much nutritional difference between the two. (We love a fresh carton of sweet summer straw-berries, but for that winter smoothie, frozen is a good alternative.)

And whenever possible, eat the peel! In addition to being a good source of fiber, the peel is packed with phytochemicals that can protect your health.

2. Runners love (and need!) carbs. But choose the right ones.

Carbohydrates are your body's favorite choice for fuel, both for the brain and working muscles. In general, runners should consume 50 to 65 percent of their calories in the form of carbs—the higher your mileage, the higher your percentage should be. This cookbook is carb-packed, and the recipes go beyond traditional pasta: You'll find quality carbs in all sorts of grains such as quinoa and rice and in pota-toes, and, yes, veggies.

Compared to refined grains, like white flours, whole grains are almost always the best choice. They're made from the entire grain, which means they include the bran, germ, and endosperm. And that's where you'll find nutritious B vitamins, iron, magnesium, selenium, and fiber—nutrients that are stripped during the refining process. The fiber in whole grains will keep you feeling fuller for longer, thanks to its ability to slow digestion. Whole grains can also help control your weight, reduce cholesterol levels, and improve heart health.

When whole grains are refined, they become much easier to digest because of the removal of fiber. That means refined carbs are a great option in the few days or hours leading up to a long run or race because your muscles will be fueled quickly and there's less chance of having an upset stomach. (While these recipes call for whole-wheat varieties, you can cer-tainly swap them out for the traditional version.)

And for runners with celiac disease or gluten allergies, there is no shortage of gluten-free recipes in this cookbook—and they are conveniently noted as such.

3. Fat is your friend: Don't avoid it, but make smart choices.

Fat has been fat-shamed over recent decades, and as a result, it has been replaced with sugar in many processed foods and recipes. But just because some-thing is low-fat or fat-free doesn't mean it's better for you. Fat is an essential part of every diet, especially a runner's diet. In addition to making food taste good, it plays a key role in keeping you healthy and, yes, boosting performance.

Fat makes you feel full, which can help you eat less. This is thanks to its nine calories per gram, compared to carbs and protein, which have just four. It is chock-full of vitamins and minerals, and when eaten alongside nutrient-rich foods (like dark leafy greens), it actually helps your body absorb certain key nutrients like vitamins A, D, E, and K.

The key is to choose the right fats. Trans fats, found in processed and fried foods, raise your levels of low-density lipoproteins (LDL, or "bad" choles-terol) while also reducing your high-density lipo-proteins (HDL, or "good" cholesterol). Too much of this fat can lead to heart disease, stroke, type 2 dia-betes, and weight gain.

Until recently, saturated fat has been shunned, which led to a low-fat and fat-free craze that's still going strong. But research is starting to show that saturated fat may provide health benefits when consumed in moderation. So while some of these recipes call for low-fat dairy to keep your calorie and saturated fat levels in check, you *can* substitute with full-fat dairy. Just keep in mind that the nutrition information listed for that recipe will no longer accurately reflect total calories, calories from fat, or grams of fat.

The best fats are unsaturated fats, which include mono- and polyunsaturated. Heart-healthy monounsaturated fats are most often found in oils like olive, canola, and sesame seed. Other sources include avocados, nuts and seeds, and nut butters. The omega-3 fatty acids found in walnuts and flaxseeds are known for their effect on brain and joint health. Runners should aim to get 20 to 35 percent of their daily calories from these healthy unsaturated fats.

4. Don't skimp on protein.

Because protein is so important for runners, a question vegetarian and vegan runners get more than any other is, "How do you get your protein?" The nutrient helps maintain lean muscle mass and repair and build new muscle tissue after hard workouts, which can cause microscopic tears and damage to muscle fibers. Studies have found that runners who consume the right amount of protein are less likely to get injured, thanks to its restorative properties.

But protein boosts more than muscle health. It is also associated with a healthy immune system, thanks to its ability to stimulate white blood cells.

And because protein takes longer to digest than simple carbohydrates, it will help you feel fuller for longer.

New research recommends that athletes, such as runners, consume 0.54 to 0.91 gram of protein per pound of body weight. Not only is that significantly more than the recommendation for non-runners, it's more than what was previously recommended for athletes. It's also important to spread your protein intake throughout the day, consuming more right before, and right after, your workouts.

So how *do* runners get their protein? There are plenty of non-meat and plant-based foods that offer high-quality protein, like eggs, dairy, nuts, tofu, lentils, and beans. Be sure to mix and match your plant protein intake so you get a complete protein, which includes nine essential amino acids required to build and maintain muscles.

5. Remember your vitamin B_{12} . . .

Non-meat-eaters generally find it easy to get their required protein intake, especially if they eat eggs and dairy. But getting enough levels of vitamin B_{12} can be more challenging. This water-soluble vitamin helps keep the nerve and blood cells healthy, make DNA, and prevent anemia.

Because it's not naturally found in plant foods, you'll want to load up on fortified foods like orange juice, milk, breads, cereals, and pastas. Be sure to read the labels to confirm which foods are fortified with B_{12}. Supplements are also an option to make up for what you're not getting in your diet, though be sure to always consult your doctor before taking any vitamin supplements.

6. ... and your iron.

Runners, regardless of their dietary preferences, are at a higher risk of developing iron deficiency than non-runners due to the effect aerobic training, like long-distance running, has on the body. Aerobic activity increases red blood cell count, and that demands a higher amount of iron.

Red meat and seafood have high levels of iron, but runners who don't eat meat can increase their iron by focusing their intake on whole grains, nuts and seeds, legumes, beans, lentils, tofu, leafy greens, and dried fruit. These foods should be eaten with vitamin C–rich foods to help increase absorption.

Before you reach for an iron supplement, find out if you're actually deficient or at risk of becoming deficient, which can be done through a simple blood test. Iron supplements can cause GI distress, and often, iron needs can be addressed through diet alone.

So how does a vegetarian or plant-based runner check off all the nutrient boxes? Read on for the best dietary sources.

Protein

Load up on these high-quality sources to help you run and recover.

BEANS AND LENTILS: Unlike animal products, most plant proteins do not offer a complete protein, which has the nine essential amino acids needed to help build and repair muscle. But as long as you eat a variety of plant-based protein sources every day, you will get all of your amino acids to form a complete protein. Most varieties of beans and lentils have 6 to 10 grams per half-cup serving.

DAIRY: For years, full-fat dairy got a bad rap. But recent research is showing that choosing full-fat yogurts and milk may reduce risk of type 2 diabetes and may be associated with lower levels of obesity. The fat in dairy helps you feel full, which helps prevent mindless snacking later in the day. If you read the labels, you'll find that flavored yogurts are often sky-high in added sugar, which adds unwanted calories and can offset the benefits of a healthy snack. As we mentioned earlier, some of our recipes do use low-fat dairy because we recognize there are many runners who are trying to keep their calories in check. You can easily substitute with the full-fat variety, but keep in mind the nutrition information listed for that recipe will no longer accurately reflect total calories, calories from fat, or grams of fat.

EGGS: New US dietary guidelines lifted the 300-milligram daily limit on dietary cholesterol (one egg has about 200 milligrams). That means eggs should be a key part of your diet. One egg provides 6 grams of protein, and the yolk is high in choline, a nutrient that promotes eye and brain health.

NUTS AND SEEDS: One ounce has 3 to 7 grams of protein, and they're high in heart-healthy fats and fiber.

QUINOA: This rising superstar is the only grain that offers a complete protein. Each cup has 8 grams.

TOFU: A go-to protein source for vegetarians and vegans, tofu packs in 10 grams of protein per half-cup serving. It's also high in isoflavone compounds, which help protect the heart.

Grains

Regardless of whether or not you're a meat-eater, runners need complex carbohydrates, like these, to keep their muscles (and brains!) fueled for the long haul.

AMARANTH: High in protein—each cooked cup has 9 grams—this unique grain is also a good source of iron and fiber.

BARLEY: Get more bang for your buck: One cup of barley has fewer calories but more fiber than quinoa, brown rice, amaranth, sorghum, millet, and wild rice.

BROWN RICE: A runner favorite, brown rice is an excellent source of bone-healthy manganese.

BULGUR: Each 1-cup serving has 25 percent of your daily fiber needs.

CORN: An excellent gluten-free grain option, corn is high in antioxidants.

FARRO: Mix with any green salad for a boost of carbohydrates, magnesium, B vitamins, and vitamin E.

OATS: This heart- and immune-healthy grain is a runner staple in the morning.

SPELT: For those sensitive to wheat, this is a good substitute that's also high in fiber.

TEFF: This iron-rich grain is a staple in Ethiopian runners' diets. 'Nuff said.

Fruits and Veggies

Hydrate and nourish your body with all sorts of fresh produce. These are some of our favorites to help power those miles.

AVOCADOS: Yes, it's a fruit! High in heart-healthy fat, avocados also provide 14 grams of fiber each.

BANANAS: This fruit is high in potassium, which plays an important role in muscle contraction and muscle health. Bananas are a great prerun and postrun snack.

BEETS: The nitrates found in beets have been shown to help boost endurance and possibly performance by helping your muscles work more efficiently.

BLACKBERRIES: The fruit's high levels of anti-oxidants may speed recovery and boost immune function.

EGGPLANT: You don't need chicken Parm when you can make eggplant Parm. Eggplants are low in calories and high in antioxidants.

KALE: This leafy green is popular for good reason: It's packed with vitamins C and K, and is an excellent source of folate. Sauté or steam to take away some of its bitter bite.

MANGOES: A cup of mango has 75 percent of your daily vitamin C needs, which can improve immune function so you have fewer sick days.

SWEET POTATOES: An excellent source of runner-friendly carbs, sweet potatoes also tout more than three times the daily requirements for vitamin A, which is important for eye health and immune function.

TOMATOES: As indicated by their red color, tomatoes have high amounts of lycopene, an antioxidant that can reduce your risk of certain cancers.

GUIDE TO
THE RECIPE KEY

At the top of each recipe, you'll find our color-coded Recipe Key. This key lets you know if the recipe meets certain training goals or dietary needs. The definitions below explain the key in detail.

PRERUN

Recipes marked **PRERUN** supply the nutrients needed to fuel a run and can be eaten about 2 hours before a workout. The majority of calories in these recipes come from carbohydrates—your body's preferred source of energy—with no more than 30 percent of calories coming from fat. These recipes also contain fewer than 20 grams of protein and about 7 grams of fiber or fewer per serving. Fat, protein, and fiber slow digestion if consumed too close to running. There are many other recipes in the cookbook not marked **PRERUN** because they fall slightly out of these guidelines, though some runners may have no problem eating these meals before a run. Because every runner has different tolerances, you should experiment to see what works for you. Remember to try any new foods long before an important race to ensure they won't upset your stomach.

RECOVERY

Recipes marked **RECOVERY** are high in protein to repair muscle tissue, and they provide some carbohydrates to restock your energy stores postrun. In general, optimal **RECOVERY** meals contain carbohydrates and protein in a ratio between 2:1 and 3:1, with at least 15 grams of protein. Some recipes labeled **RECOVERY** may contain slightly fewer or more carbohydrates than the suggested ratio. Regardless of the amount of carbohydrate a recipe contains, meals can also earn the **RECOVERY** label if they provide 15 to 25 grams of protein or more per serving. Fat and fiber content were not taken into consideration, since they do not significantly affect recovery.

FAST

These recipes can be prepared in 30 minutes or less.

VEGAN

These recipes contain no animal products at all. They exclude eggs, dairy, and honey.

LOW-CALORIE

This category is provided for runners who may be trying to lose weight. These recipes contain 400 calories or fewer per serving—or 20 percent of your total calorie needs based on a 2,000-calorie daily diet.

GLUTEN-FREE

Recipes marked **GLUTEN-FREE** do not contain gluten, a protein found in wheat, barley, and rye. Many of these recipes use naturally gluten-free products, including vegetable broths; eggs; gluten-free grains, such as corn, rice, quinoa, and oats; and spices or spice blends, such as curry. However, because even naturally gluten-free products can sometimes be contaminated with trace amounts of gluten, it's key that runners who have an extreme sensitivity, such as those with celiac disease, check product labels. Bob's Red Mill offers an extensive line of grains and flours that are certified gluten-free, while broths made by Pacific Natural Foods, Imagine Foods, and Kitchen Basics are gluten-free. Bottled and jarred condiments (such as soy sauce) that typically contain gluten are not used in the **GLUTEN-FREE** recipes. However, many of these products are available in a gluten-free version, which can be substituted for the traditional product. Research has not found any performance or weight loss benefit tied to gluten-free diets.

ALLERGEN-FREE

Recipes marked **ALLERGEN-FREE** are free of all eight common allergens: milk, eggs, fish, crustacean shellfish, tree nuts, peanuts, wheat, and soy.

(Note that all recipes in this vegetarian cookbook are also free of fish and shellfish.)

1 BREAKFAST

BAKED GOODS

Fresh Fruit Scones 18

Walnut Sweet Potato Bread 20

Zucchini Bread 23

"Baked" Granola Apples 24

CEREALS

Quinoa Breakfast Porridge 21

Slow-Cooker Apple-Cinnamon
Oatmeal 26

Granola with Toasted Almonds
and Cherries 29

PANCAKES, WAFFLES, AND TOAST

Buckwheat Pancakes 27

Whole Wheat, Flaxseed and
Blueberry Pancakes 30

Pumpkin Ricotta Waffles 33

Avocado Toast 34

PB & Homemade Jelly Toast 36

EGGS

Egg with Grits and Mushrooms 37

Baked Egg in Avocado 39

"Eggy" Tofu Scramble 40

Spinach and Feta Frittata 41

Pesto Egg Cups 42

Breakfast Tacos 44

BOWLS

Greek Yogurt Bowl 45

Berry Tasty Smoothie Bowl 47

Mango Tango Smoothie Bowl 48

FRESH FRUIT SCONES

Using whatever fruit is in season is a natural way to add a hint of sweetness, and adding whole wheat flour makes this breakfast treat a little more nutritious thanks to its fiber content. Fuel your morning run with one, or have it postrun with 1 cup of Greek yogurt for added protein, and a cup of coffee or tea.

MAKES 8 SCONES // TOTAL TIME: 1 HOUR 10 MINUTES

1¾ cups all-purpose flour
½ cup whole wheat flour
½ cup sugar
1½ tablespoons baking powder
¾ teaspoon baking soda
6 tablespoons cold unsalted butter, cut into pieces
1 cup buttermilk, divided
1 teaspoon vanilla extract
1 cup fresh fruit, such as diced peaches, whole blueberries, chopped cherries, or diced mango

Preheat the oven to 350°F. Line the bottom of a 9" round cake pan with parchment paper or coat the bottom with cooking spray.

In a large bowl, combine the all-purpose flour, whole wheat flour, sugar, baking powder, and baking soda. Cut in the butter using a pastry blender, fork, or two butter knives (moving the knives in opposite directions) until the butter pieces are pea-size and coated with flour. (This creates a flakier scone.)

In a small bowl, combine ¾ cup of the buttermilk and the vanilla. Pour the buttermilk mixture into the dry ingredients and stir until combined. If the dough seems dry, add the remaining ¼ cup buttermilk as needed. Add the fruit and mix until combined.

Transfer the dough to the cake pan and gently pat it into the pan. Using a butter knife, gently score the top of the dough into 8 pieces (like a pie), taking care not to cut all the way through. Bake for 35 to 40 minutes, or until the scones are golden brown. Let them cool on a wire rack for about 15 minutes, then cut into 8 pieces along the scored lines.

NUTRITION PER SCONE   277 calories / 44 g carbohydrates / 2 g fiber / 16 g sugars / 5 g protein / 9 g total fat / 6 g saturated fat / 454 mg sodium

WALNUT SWEET POTATO BREAD

Perfect for a prerun nibble, this nutrient-rich snack will power your morning miles. Walnuts are packed with good-for-you omega-3s, and sweet potatoes will boost your immune system with their antioxidants. For a hint of sweetness, bake with a dried fruit, like dried cranberries, top with a little jam, or smear with nut butter for added protein.

MAKES 10 SERVINGS (1 LOAF, 10 SLICES) // TOTAL TIME: 1 HOUR 45 MINUTES

2	large sweet potatoes
1	cup rolled oats
1	cup whole wheat flour
1	teaspoon baking powder
1	teaspoon baking soda
1	teaspoon salt
1	tablespoon ground cinnamon
½	teaspoon ground nutmeg
⅔	cup maple syrup
1½	teaspoons vanilla extract
½	cup canola oil
2	eggs
1	cup chopped walnuts
½	to ¾ cup chopped dried fruit (optional)

Preheat the oven to 400°F. Wrap the sweet potatoes in foil and bake for 45 minutes, or until softened. When cool enough to handle, scrape the flesh from the skins and mash. You should have about 1¼ cups of mashed sweet potato.

Reduce the heat to 350°F and grease a 9" × 5" loaf pan. In a medium bowl, combine the oats, flour, baking powder, baking soda, salt, cinnamon, and nutmeg.

In a large bowl, combine the maple syrup, vanilla, oil, and eggs and mix well. Slowly add the dry ingredients to the wet ingredients, mixing just until combined. Fold in the walnuts and the dried fruit, if using.

Pour the batter into the loaf pan and bake for 35 to 40 minutes, or until a toothpick inserted into the center comes out clean.

PRO TIP

Running short on time? Cook your sweet potatoes in the microwave. To microwave a whole sweet potato, prick it all over with a fork and microwave on high for 8 to 10 minutes, or until tender.

NUTRITION PER SERVING (1 SLICE)

279 calories / 37 g carbohydrates / 4 g fiber / 17 g sugars / 5 g protein / 13 g total fat / 1.5 g saturated fat / 437 mg sodium

QUINOA BREAKFAST PORRIDGE

Warm up after a chilly fall run with this gluten-free porridge that's high in protein. While we recommended it eaten with pear, you can substitute whatever fruit is in season. Go with maple syrup instead of honey to make this breakfast vegan.

MAKES 1 SERVING // TOTAL TIME: 10 MINUTES

½ **cup cooked quinoa**

½ **cup unsweetened almond milk**

⅔ **cup diced fresh pear, plus more for garnish**

½ **teaspoon ground cinnamon**

¼ **teaspoon ground allspice**

Pinch of ground nutmeg

Pinch of sea salt

¼ **cup walnuts, toasted**

Honey or maple syrup, to taste

In a small saucepan, combine the quinoa, almond milk, pear, spices, and salt and bring to a gentle boil over medium-high heat. Reduce the heat to a simmer and stir until thickened to your liking. For oatmeal consistency, simmer about 5 minutes.

Sprinkle with the walnuts, add a few slices of pear, and enjoy warm. Drizzle with honey or maple syrup for a sweet finish.

NUTRITION PER SERVING

389 calories / 43 g carbohydrates / 9 g fiber / 12 g sugars / 10 g protein / 23 g total fat / 2 g saturated fat / 197 mg sodium

ZUCCHINI BREAD

This family recipe was modified to cut back on sugar and fat, using a little bit of brown sugar and unsweetened applesauce. Walnuts are one of the best brain foods, and they're high in vitamin E, a powerful antioxidant. Have a slice with nut butter after your run. Or skip the run and pair with coffee on a lazy Sunday morning (we won't tell!).

MAKES 20 SERVINGS (2 LOAVES, 10 SLICES EACH) // TOTAL TIME: 1 HOUR 45 MINUTES, PLUS COOLING TIME

3	large eggs
1	medium zucchini (12 to 14 ounces), grated
1	cup brown sugar
⅔	cup canola oil
⅓	cup unsweetened applesauce
1	tablespoon vanilla extract
2	cups all-purpose flour
1	cup whole wheat flour
1	cup chopped walnuts
1	tablespoon ground cinnamon
1	teaspoon salt
1	teaspoon baking soda
1	teaspoon ground ginger
1	teaspoon ground nutmeg
¼	teaspoon baking powder

Preheat the oven to 325°F. Generously grease two 9" × 5" loaf pans.

In a large bowl, beat the eggs. Stir in the zucchini, brown sugar, oil, applesauce, and vanilla.

In a medium bowl, combine the all-purpose flour, whole wheat flour, walnuts, cinnamon, salt, baking soda, ginger, nutmeg, and baking powder. Stir into the zucchini mixture until completely combined. Divide the batter evenly between the loaf pans.

Bake for 1 hour, or until golden on top and a toothpick inserted into the center comes out clean. Cool in the pans on wire racks for 15 minutes. Remove from the pans and let cool completely.

NUTRITION PER SERVING (1 SLICE)

165 calories / 27 g carbohydrates / 2 g fiber / 12 g sugars / 4 g protein / 5 g total fat / 1 g saturated fat / 201 mg sodium

"BAKED" GRANOLA APPLES

Using the microwave instead of the oven "bakes" these apples with steam until they're perfectly tender. Braeburn, Cortland, and Rome apples work just as well as Gala. Use a spoon or melon baller to core the halved apples. Serve with a scoop of plain Greek yogurt for a protein and calcium boost.

MAKES 4 SERVINGS // TOTAL TIME: 10 MINUTES

2   large crisp apples, such as Gala, halved and cored

2   tablespoons chopped dried tart cherries

1   tablespoon packed light brown sugar

¼   teaspoon ground cinnamon

⅛   teaspoon ground nutmeg

4   teaspoons butter

½   cup granola, such as Granola with Toasted Almonds and Cherries (page 29)

In a microwaveable dish, arrange the apple halves cut side up. Top each apple half evenly with the cherries and brown sugar. Sprinkle with the cinnamon and nutmeg and dot evenly with the butter.

Cover the apples with a microwaveable dome lid. Microwave on high power for 4 minutes, or until the apples are tender.

Transfer the apples to serving bowls and sprinkle each apple half evenly with granola. Drizzle any juices remaining in the cooking dish on top.

NUTRITION PER SERVING

194 calories / 30 g carbohydrates / 5 g fiber / 20 g sugars / 3 g protein / 8 g total fat / 3 g saturated fat / 40 mg sodium

SLOW-COOKER APPLE-CINNAMON OATMEAL

When you cook these oats the night before a long run, you'll wake up to the smell of apple and cinnamon—and may be tempted to skip your run altogether. But trust us: Get your miles in, and *then* refuel with a piping-hot bowl of heart-healthy oats. Top with banana for muscle-friendly potassium, or mix in some nut butter for a boost of protein. If you have leftovers, reheat them on the stovetop with a splash of milk.

MAKES 4 SERVINGS // TOTAL TIME: 10 MINUTES, PLUS 8 HOURS COOKING TIME

1 cup steel-cut oats

½ cup apple cider

½ cup heavy cream,
    half-and-half, or milk

3½ cups water

1 large apple, half grated,
    the other half chopped

2 tablespoons maple syrup

2 tablespoons lightly
    packed dark brown sugar

½ teaspoon ground
    cinnamon

    Pinch of kosher salt,
    or to taste

In a slow cooker, combine the oats, cider, cream, water, grated and chopped apple, maple syrup, brown sugar, cinnamon, and salt. Cover and cook on low for 8 to 10 hours.

NUTRITION PER SERVING

337 calories / 52 g carbohydrates / 6 g fiber / 22 g sugars / 7 g protein / 14 g total fat / 7.5 g saturated fat / 53 mg sodium

BUCKWHEAT PANCAKES

Unlike traditional white flour, buckwheat flour provides fiber, manganese, magnesium, and copper. Plus, it makes a very hearty pancake. Serve with buckwheat honey for strong flavor or top with fresh fruit and pure maple syrup.

MAKES 7 SERVINGS (14 PANCAKES) // TOTAL TIME: 15 MINUTES

½ cup whole wheat flour
½ cup buckwheat flour
1 teaspoon baking powder
½ teaspoon salt
1 large egg
1 cup whole milk
¼ cup water
2 tablespoons honey
1 teaspoon butter

In a large bowl, combine the flours. Whisk in the baking powder and salt.

In a small bowl, beat together the egg, milk, water, and honey. Stir the wet ingredients into the flour mixture until just moistened, taking care not to overmix. The batter will be thin.

In a griddle or skillet over medium heat, melt the butter. Ladle the batter by scant ¼ cupfuls onto the griddle and cook, turning once, until golden brown on both sides. Transfer to a plate. Repeat with the remaining batter.

NUTRITION PER SERVING (2 PANCAKES)

125 calories / 19 g carbohydrates / 2 g fiber / 7 g sugars / 4 g protein / 4 g total fat / 1 g saturated fat / 263 mg sodium

GRANOLA WITH TOASTED ALMONDS AND CHERRIES

Granola and breakfast cereals are often packed with added sugar, so making your own granola is the best way to control the amount of sugar that goes into it. Using a little honey and brown sugar can go a long way, or you can cut back even more and add a few dashes of cinnamon for flavor instead.

MAKES 10 SERVINGS (5 CUPS) // TOTAL TIME: 50 MINUTES

- 3 **cups quick-cooking oats**
- ½ **cup sliced almonds**
- 2 **tablespoons flaxseeds**
- 2 **tablespoons sesame seeds**
- ¼ **teaspoon salt**
- ⅓ **cup honey**
- 1 **tablespoon turbinado sugar or light brown sugar**
- 1 **tablespoon extra-light olive oil**
- 1 **teaspoon vanilla extract**
- 1 **cup chopped dried cherries**

Preheat the oven to 300°F. On a large rimmed baking sheet, combine the oats, almonds, flaxseeds, sesame seeds, and salt. Bake for 30 minutes, or until the oats and almonds are toasted and fragrant. Increase the heat to 350°F.

Meanwhile, in a small saucepan, combine the honey, turbinado sugar, and oil. Cook over medium heat for 1 minute, or until the sugar has melted. Remove from the heat and stir in the vanilla.

Drizzle the honey mixture over the oats and stir to coat. Bake, stirring occasionally, for 10 minutes, or until the oats are crispy. With a spoon, break up any clumps. Stir in the cherries. Cool completely before storing in an airtight container.

NUTRITION PER SERVING (½ CUP)

243 calories / 40 g carbohydrates / 7 g fiber / 17 g sugars / 6 g protein / 7 g total fat / 0.5 g saturated fat / 60 mg sodium

WHOLE WHEAT, FLAXSEED, AND BLUEBERRY PANCAKES

Once my husband discovered the fluffiest pancake recipe, we would make them once a week, without fail, after long runs. And then we started experimenting: What if we used part whole wheat flour? What if we added fruit? What if we went entirely whole wheat and added ground flaxseeds? Pretty soon we revolutionized our favorite fluffy, white-flour recipe to one packed with fiber, healthy fats, and antioxidants. And yes, they're still fluffy—and they taste great. We top them with pure maple syrup and homemade jams. This recipe makes 8 pancakes and serves four, but two people could easily polish them off.

MAKES 4 SERVINGS (8 PANCAKES) // TOTAL TIME: 20 MINUTES

¾	**cup whole milk**
2	**tablespoons apple cider vinegar**
1	**cup whole wheat flour**
2	**tablespoons sugar**
1	**tablespoon ground flaxseeds**
1	**teaspoon baking powder**
½	**teaspoon baking soda**
½	**teaspoon salt**
1	**egg**
2	**tablespoons unsalted butter, melted and cooled, plus more for the skillet**
½	**cup fresh or frozen blueberries**
	Pure maple syrup or jam, for serving

In a small bowl, combine the milk and vinegar. Let sit for 5 minutes.

In a large bowl, combine the flour, sugar, flaxseed meal, baking powder, baking soda, and salt. Mix well.

In a separate small bowl, whisk together the egg and butter. Add the milk mixture and whisk to combine. Pour the wet mixture into the dry ingredients and whisk until combined. Gently stir in the blueberries.

In a large skillet over medium-high heat, melt ½ to 1 tablespoon butter. Pour the batter onto the skillet, making 4 pancakes (reserving half the batter). Cook for 2 to 3 minutes, or until bubbles start to form on the tops and the bottoms are slightly brown. Turn the pancakes and cook for 2 to 3 minutes, or until the bottoms are slightly brown. Transfer the pancakes to a plate. Repeat with the remaining batter, adding more butter to the skillet if needed. Top with your favorite maple syrup or jam.

NUTRITION PER SERVING (2 PANCAKES)

274 calories / 35 g carbohydrates / 4 g fiber / 11 g sugars / 8 g protein / 13 g total fat / 7 g saturated fat / 610 mg sodium

PUMPKIN RICOTTA WAFFLES

You don't need to spend your lazy weekend morning (this means the day you're not running!) prepping a healthy, tasty breakfast. Whole grain toaster waffles are a quick way to make a fiber-rich and nutritious breakfast. Nuts and ricotta cheese add some healthy fat to keep you feeling full.

MAKES 1 SERVING // TOTAL TIME: 5 MINUTES

2	whole grain toaster waffles
¼	cup canned unsweetened pumpkin puree
2	tablespoons ricotta cheese
1	tablespoon maple syrup
⅛	teaspoon pumpkin pie spice
1	tablespoon chopped pecans

Heat the waffles in a toaster.

Meanwhile, in a microwaveable bowl, stir together the pumpkin puree, ricotta, maple syrup, and pumpkin pie spice until thoroughly combined. Microwave on high power for 30 seconds, or until warmed through.

Spread the pumpkin mixture on the toasted waffles. Sprinkle with the pecans.

NUTRITION PER SERVING

373 calories / 47 g carbohydrates / 4 g fiber / 21 g sugars / 12 g protein / 16 g total fat / 4.5 g saturated fat / 308 mg sodium

AVOCADO TOAST

Avocado toast is an easy, nutrient-filled breakfast high in heart-healthy fat and vitamin C. For a hit of protein (and to up your Instagram game), top with a fried egg.

MAKES 2 SERVINGS // TOTAL TIME: 5 MINUTES

2   slices whole grain or multigrain bread
1   avocado, halved, pitted, and peeled
1   teaspoon fresh lemon or lime juice
    Salt and ground black pepper, to taste

Toast the bread slices.

In a small bowl, combine the avocado and lemon or lime juice. Using a fork, mash together until almost smooth. Spread over the toast.

Season with salt and pepper.

NUTRITION PER SERVING 205 calories / 21 g carbohydrates / 8 g fiber / 2 g sugars / 5 g protein / 13 g total fat / 2 g saturated fat / 396 mg sodium

PB & HOMEMADE JELLY TOAST

Peanut butter and jelly is a runner favorite: It's a great source of simple carbs (for the brain and muscles) thanks to bread and jelly, and high in protein from peanut butter. Adding chia seeds to this classic boosts fiber and, according to a 2014 study, may reduce mortality from various diseases.

MAKES 4 SERVINGS // TOTAL TIME: 10 MINUTES, PLUS COOLING TIME

1½ cups raspberries

2 tablespoons chia seeds

1 tablespoon honey

1 tablespoon fresh lemon juice

4 slices whole wheat bread, toasted

4 tablespoons peanut butter

In a small saucepan over medium-low heat, cook the raspberries for 5 minutes, or until softened and broken down. Add the chia seeds, honey, and lemon juice, and cook, stirring occasionally, for 2 minutes. Remove from the heat and let the jam cool.

Top each slice of toast with 1 tablespoon peanut butter and ¼ cup jam. Store any remaining jam, covered, in the refrigerator for up to 5 days.

NUTRITION PER SERVING

230 calories / 27 g carbohydrates / 8 g fiber / 9 g sugars / 9 g protein / 11 g total fat / 2 g saturated fat / 188 mg sodium

EGG WITH GRITS AND MUSHROOMS

Mix up your traditional eggs with grits and shiitake mushrooms. The mushrooms are a good source of B vitamins, which can help your body create energy from carbs. If you ran long, add another egg for a boost of protein.

MAKES 1 SERVING // TOTAL TIME: 10 MINUTES

¼ **cup instant grits**

¼ **teaspoon minced garlic**

3 **medium shiitake mushroom caps, sliced**

¼ **cup low-sodium vegetable broth**

1 **large egg**
   Salt and ground black pepper, to taste

Cook the grits according to the package directions, stirring in the garlic with the water. Set aside.

Meanwhile, in a small nonstick skillet over medium-high heat, cook the mushrooms with the vegetable broth, stirring occasionally, until most of the liquid has been absorbed. Stir the mushrooms into the grits and wipe out the skillet with a paper towel.

Coat the skillet with cooking spray and fry the egg sunny-side up over low to medium heat. Top the grits and mushrooms with the egg and season with salt and pepper.

NUTRITION PER SERVING

202 calories / 27 g carbohydrates / 3 g fiber / 2 g sugars / 10 g protein / 6 g total fat / 2 g saturated fat / 696 mg sodium

BAKED EGG IN AVOCADO

Few things go better together than avocado and eggs. Cut out the toast middleman by baking your egg right inside the avocado for a protein- and healthy-fat-packed breakfast.

MAKES 2 SERVINGS // TOTAL TIME: 20 MINUTES

1   ripe avocado, halved and
    pitted
    Hot sauce, to taste
    (optional)
2   eggs
    Salt and ground black
    pepper, to taste

Preheat the oven to 425°F. Scoop out a spoonful of flesh from each avocado half to make room for the egg. Slice a small piece from the rounded bottom of each avocado half so they will sit flat and steadily. Place the avocado halves on a baking sheet.

Drizzle hot sauce to taste (if using) into the avocado halves. Crack an egg into each half—don't worry if the whites spill out a little. Sprinkle with salt and pepper to taste.

Bake for 15 minutes, or until the eggs are cooked through.

NUTRITION PER SERVING

185 calories / 6 g carbohydrates / 5 g fiber / 0 g sugars / 8 g protein / 15 g total fat / 3 g saturated fat / 222 mg sodium

"EGGY" TOFU SCRAMBLE

Regardless of your animal-product preference, using tofu for your morning scramble instead of eggs is a nutritious way to change up your breakfast. Tofu, a high-quality protein, can be spiced up with whatever you're cooking, and thanks to the nutritional yeast in this recipe, you'll get a great savory flavor. Choose a tofu brand fortified with vitamin B_{12}, a nutrient most commonly found in chicken and eggs. Toss in any leftover cooked vegetables you have on hand for a nutrient boost.

MAKES 2 SERVINGS // TOTAL TIME: 20 MINUTES

2   teaspoons ground cumin
½   teaspoon ground turmeric
    Pinch of chili powder
    (optional)
½   teaspoon salt
¼   teaspoon ground black
    pepper
3   tablespoons water
2   tablespoons canola oil
1   small onion, chopped
3   cloves garlic, minced
1   package (14 to 16 ounces)
    firm tofu, drained and
    crumbled into bite-size
    pieces
3   tablespoons nutritional
    yeast

In a small bowl, combine the cumin, turmeric, chili powder (if using), salt, pepper, and water. Stir well. Set aside.

In a large skillet over medium-high heat, heat the oil. Add the onion and garlic and cook for 2 to 3 minutes, or until soft. Add the tofu and cook for 10 minutes, stirring often with a metal spatula so the tofu doesn't stick to the pan.

Add the spice mixture and nutritional yeast and stir gently to combine. If the pan is too dry, add a few teaspoons of water. Cook for 1 to 2 minutes. Serve warm.

NUTRITION PER SERVING   358 calories / 14 g carbohydrates / 6 g fiber / 2 g sugars / 25 g protein / 24 g total fat / 2 g saturated fat / 600 mg sodium

SPINACH AND FETA FRITTATA

Frittatas are one of the best ways to sneak in leafy greens like spinach. A true superfood, spinach is high in vitamins A and K, B vitamins, folate, and iron. If you can't find baby spinach, use 1¼ pounds large spinach and discard the tough stems. Slice the leaves crosswise into thin shreds and wash in a bowl of water, swishing to dislodge any sand. Dry in a salad spinner or pat dry with paper towels.

MAKES 6 SERVINGS // TOTAL TIME: 20 MINUTES

- 3 tablespoons olive oil, divided
- ¼ cup chopped onion
- 2 cloves garlic, minced
- 1 pound baby spinach leaves
- 4 eggs
- 4 egg whites
- ¼ cup very finely crumbled soft whole grain bread crumbs (½ slice)
- 2 tablespoons chopped fresh basil
- 2 teaspoons grated lemon zest
- ½ teaspoon ground black pepper
- 1 cup crumbled feta cheese (4 ounces)

Preheat the oven to 450°F.

In a large ovenproof skillet over medium heat, heat 1 tablespoon of the oil. Add the onion and garlic and cook for 5 minutes, or until soft. Add the spinach and stir until wilted. Remove from the skillet and cover to keep warm.

In a medium bowl, beat together the whole eggs and egg whites. Beat in the bread crumbs, basil, lemon zest, and pepper.

In the same skillet over medium heat, heat the remaining 2 tablespoons of the oil. Stir the spinach mixture and the feta into the egg mixture, then pour into the skillet. Cook the eggs, lifting up the bottom with a spatula to allow the uncooked egg to run underneath, for 1 to 2 minutes, or until set.

Transfer the skillet to the oven and bake for 5 to 6 minutes, or until the top of the frittata is puffy and set. Cut into 6 wedges to serve.

NUTRITION PER SERVING

243 calories / 11 g carbohydrates / 4 g fiber / 2 g sugars / 13 g protein / 15 g total fat / 6 g saturated fat / 517 mg sodium

PESTO EGG CUPS

Your muffin pan is good for a lot more than just muffins—like these perfectly portioned egg cups. Tomatoes are a good source of lycopene, an antioxidant that may help ward off cancer. And when they're paired with pesto, you've got a breakfast that will transport you to Italy. *Buon appetito!*

MAKES 4 SERVINGS (12 EGG CUPS) // TOTAL TIME: 30 MINUTES

8	**eggs**
⅓	**cup sour cream**
⅓	**cup chopped sun-dried tomatoes**
3	**tablespoons pesto**
½	**teaspoon salt**
¼	**teaspoon red pepper flakes**
1	**tablespoon chopped fresh chives**

Preheat the oven to 375°F. Grease a muffin pan. In a large bowl, whisk together the eggs, sour cream, sun-dried tomatoes, pesto, salt, and red pepper flakes.

Divide the egg mixture evenly among the muffin cups and bake for 20 minutes, or until the eggs are set. Serve topped with the chives.

NUTRITION PER SERVING (3 EGG CUPS)

244 calories / 5 g carbohydrates / 1 g fiber / 3 g sugars / 16 g protein / 18 g total fat / 6.5 g saturated fat / 546 mg sodium

BREAKFAST TACOS

US dietary guidelines have lifted the daily cholesterol limit of 300 milligrams, meaning you can safely go for the whole egg (200 milligrams) in one meal. But if you're watching calories and saturated fat, skip the yolk and use egg whites, which still offer quality protein.

MAKES 1 SERVING (4 TACOS) // TOTAL TIME: 10 MINUTES

4	corn tortillas (6" diameter)
4	egg whites, scrambled and cooked
½	cup fresh baby spinach leaves
¼	cup salsa
¼	cup sliced avocado

Warm the tortillas according to package directions, then fill evenly with the scrambled egg whites, spinach, salsa, and avocado.

NUTRITION PER SERVING   361 calories / 53 g carbohydrates / 10 g fiber / 5 g sugars / 22 g protein / 9 g total fat / 1.5 g saturated fat / 735 mg sodium

GREEK YOGURT BOWL

Using Greek yogurt instead of milk with your granola ups your protein (and probiotic) intake. It'll also make you feel fuller for longer. But be wary: *Greek yogurt* is not a regulated term, meaning anything can be called "Greek." Read the ingredient list and make sure that "live and active cultures" are specifically listed and the strains are specified. To keep your sugar count down, go for the plain variety and add fruit or honey for sweetness. Selecting a full-fat variety is also a great way to stay full and help your body absorb fat-soluble vitamins like D and K.

MAKES 1 SERVING // TOTAL TIME: 5 MINUTES

1   **cup full-fat plain Greek yogurt**
¼   **cup fresh raspberries**
¼   **cup granola**
2   **teaspoons honey**
1   **teaspoon ground flaxseeds**

In a bowl, combine the yogurt, raspberries, granola, honey, and flaxseeds.

NUTRITION PER SERVING

520 calories / 39 g carbohydrates / 5 g fiber / 26 g sugars / 20 g protein / 32 g total fat / 19.5 g saturated fat / 74 mg sodium

BERRY TASTY SMOOTHIE BOWL

You can't go wrong with smoothies and toppings, and with this recipe, you can have both. Adding protein powder and healthy fats found in seeds and coconut to your smoothie will help fuel your muscles and keep you feeling full until lunch.

MAKES 1 SERVING // TOTAL TIME: 5 MINUTES

SMOOTHIE

- 1 **frozen banana**
- ½ **cup frozen mixed berries**
- ½ **cup frozen cherries**
- ½ **cup water**
- 1 **scoop plant-based protein powder**
- 1 **tablespoon natural almond butter**

TOPPINGS

- 1 **tablespoon dried tart cherries**
- 1 **tablespoon raw hulled pumpkin seeds**
- 1 **tablespoon dried goji berries**
- 1½ **teaspoons unsweetened shredded coconut**
- ¼ **cup frozen mixed berries**

In a blender, combine the banana, berries, frozen cherries, water, protein powder, and almond butter. Blend until smooth.

Pour the smoothie into a wide bowl. Top with the dried cherries, pumpkin seeds, goji berries, coconut, and mixed berries.

NUTRITION PER SERVING 573 calories / 74 g carbohydrates / 21 g fiber / 38 g sugars / 23 g protein / 22 g total fat / 6.5 g saturated fat / 34 mg sodium

MANGO TANGO SMOOTHIE BOWL

Start your day with a refreshing kick thanks to the mango and cayenne pepper in this trendy smoothie bowl. The cashew topping adds a nice crunch and some healthy fat.

MAKES 1 SERVING // TOTAL TIME: 5 MINUTES

SMOOTHIE

½ **cup frozen chopped mango**

½ **frozen chopped banana**

⅓ **cup almond milk**

½ **cup silken tofu**

1 **teaspoon grated lime zest**

⅛ **teaspoon cayenne pepper**

TOPPINGS

1 **tablespoon chopped roasted cashews**

1 **kiwifruit, peeled and sliced**

1 **teaspoon honey**

In a blender, combine the mango, banana, almond milk, tofu, lime zest, and cayenne pepper. Blend until smooth.

Pour the smoothie into a chilled bowl and top with the cashews, kiwifruit, and honey.

NUTRITION PER SERVING

408 calories / 58 g carbohydrates / 9 g fiber / 39 g sugars / 11 g protein / 18 g total fat / 9.5 g saturated fat / 114 mg sodium

2

SMOOTHIES & DRINKS

SMOOTHIES

Cranberry Beet Smoothie 54

Green Smoothie 55

Sweet Potato Puree Smoothie 56

Watermelon Smoothie 57

PB&J Smoothie 58

Postrun Smoothie 58

Espresso Almond Smoothie 59

DRINKS

Ginger-Spiked Peach Fizz 60

Iced Spiced Cocoa Latte 61

Honeydew Lime Cooler 62

Mexican Coffee 64

Cardamom-Ginger Chai Tea 65

Hot Gingered Cider with
    Lady Apples 67

Passion Fruit, Pineapple, and
    Mint Cooler 68

Cranberry Beet Smoothie

(page 54)

Green Smoothie

(page 55)

Sweet Potato Puree Smoothie

(page 56)

Watermelon
Smoothie
(page 57)

Espresso Almond
Smoothie
(page 59)

CRANBERRY BEET SMOOTHIE

Before you balk at drinking beets and spinach, know that the fruit, honey, and spices will make this a sweet (but not too sweet) performance booster. Beets and spinach contain nitrates, which have been shown to improve your body's ability to use oxygen so you can run more efficiently. Bottoms up!

MAKES 1 SERVING // TOTAL TIME: 5 MINUTES

1	cup water
1	small beet, chopped
½	cup fresh cranberries
1	cup spinach
1	teaspoon honey
1	teaspoon minced fresh ginger
½	teaspoon ground allspice
1	cup ice cubes

In a blender, combine the water, beet, cranberries, spinach, honey, ginger, allspice, and ice cubes. Blend until smooth.

NUTRITION PER SERVING   79 calories / 19 g carbohydrates / 5 g fiber / 12 g sugars / 2 g protein / 0 g total fat / 0 g saturated fat / 81 mg sodium

GREEN SMOOTHIE

Ginger can help calm GI distress (making it your secret weapon before a big race), and a small study found that a ginger supplement may help reduce exercise-induced muscle soreness.

MAKES 2 SERVINGS // TOTAL TIME: 5 MINUTES

1   **pear, cored and diced**

2   **cups vanilla soy or almond milk**

2   **cups baby spinach leaves**

2   **teaspoons fresh lemon juice**

1   **teaspoon grated fresh ginger**

¼   **teaspoon ground cardamom**

In a blender, combine the pear, milk, spinach, lemon juice, ginger, and cardamom. Blend until smooth. Divide between two glasses.

NUTRITION PER SERVING   164 calories / 26 g carbohydrates / 5 g fiber / 16 g sugars / 7 g protein / 4 g total fat / 0.5 g saturated fat / 127 mg sodium

SWEET POTATO PUREE SMOOTHIE

If you need a meal to go, this smoothie has a runner-approved balance of carbs, fiber, protein, and fat—plus loads of immune-boosting vitamin A. Kefir is also an excellent source of probiotics, which can improve your gut health.

MAKES 1 SERVING // TOTAL TIME: 5 MINUTES

1   cup low-fat plain kefir
½   cup peeled cooked sweet potato, cooled
¼   cup canned navy beans, rinsed and drained
1   tablespoon chopped walnuts
½   teaspoon vanilla extract
⅛   teaspoon ground cloves
½   banana, chopped and frozen

In a blender, combine the kefir, sweet potato, beans, walnuts, vanilla, cloves, and banana. Blend until smooth.

NUTRITION PER SERVING

407 calories / 69 g carbohydrates / 9 g fiber / 17 g sugars / 20 g protein / 7 g total fat / 2 g saturated fat / 463 mg sodium

WATERMELON SMOOTHIE

Iced watermelon is one of the most refreshing postrun treats out there (not to mention that the summer fruit is packed with potassium to help with muscle function). Add milk and you've got some of your postrun recovery protein. This recipe calls for fat-free, but whole milk is also a great option and will help you feel full longer. Sensitive to dairy? Try almond milk. Pair this with a nut butter sandwich for the extra calories you'll need after a hard run.

MAKES 2 SERVINGS // TOTAL TIME: 5 MINUTES

2   cups chopped watermelon
¼   cup fat-free milk
2   cups ice, plus more if
    needed

In a blender, combine the watermelon and milk. Blend for 15 seconds, or until smooth. Add the ice and blend for 20 seconds, or to your desired consistency. If needed, add more ice and blend for 10 seconds.

NUTRITION PER SERVING

56 calories / 13 g carbohydrates / 1 g fiber / 11 g sugars / 2 g protein / 0 g total fat / 0 g saturated fat / 21 mg sodium

PB&J SMOOTHIE

POSTRUN SMOOTHIE

Hemp milk, made from hemp seeds, is a good source of omega-3s and has all nine essential amino acids your body needs to build protein. Flaxseeds are another great source of healthy fat and fiber.

Start your morning with this potassium-packed breakfast. The fat in nut butter helps improve the absorption of nutrients found in kale, such as vitamin K. Opt for plain Greek yogurt to keep your sugar count down.

MAKES 2 SERVINGS // TOTAL TIME: 5 MINUTES

MAKES 1 SERVING // TOTAL TIME: 5 MINUTES

½ cup unsweetened hemp milk

3 tablespoons unsweetened natural peanut butter

2 tablespoons ground flaxseeds

¾ cup frozen red grapes

½ frozen banana

In a blender, combine the hemp milk, peanut butter, flaxseeds, grapes, and banana. Blend until smooth. Divide between two glasses.

½ cup fresh strawberries, hulled

1 cup kale leaves

½ cup Greek yogurt

½ banana

1½ teaspoons nut butter

1 tablespoon chia seeds

¼ cup water

In a blender, combine the strawberries, kale, yogurt, banana, nut butter, and chia seeds. Blend until smooth. Add the water, plus more as needed, until you reach your desired consistency.

NUTRITION PER SERVING

PB&J SMOOTHIE: 318 calories / 34 g carbohydrates / 5 g fiber / 21 g sugars / 9 g protein / 17 g total fat / 2 g saturated fat / 154 mg sodium

POSTRUN SMOOTHIE: 285 calories / 36 g carbohydrates / 9 g fiber / 17 g sugars / 17 g protein / 11 g total fat / 3 g saturated fat / 103 mg sodium

THE RUNNER'S WORLD VEGETARIAN COOKBOOK

ESPRESSO ALMOND SMOOTHIE

You really can't go wrong with a chocolate-coffee combo. Kick-start your workout (and your day) with this smoothie, which is full of protein and caffeine. The latter has been shown to boost performance by making hard efforts feel easier.

MAKES 1 SERVING // TOTAL TIME: 5 MINUTES

1   banana, sliced and frozen
½   cup unsweetened almond milk
2   tablespoons cooled brewed espresso
1   teaspoon unsweetened cocoa powder
1   tablespoon almond butter

In a blender, combine the banana, almond milk, espresso, cocoa powder, and almond butter. Blend until smooth.

NUTRITION PER SERVING

228 calories / 32 g carbohydrates / 6 g fiber / 15 g sugars / 5 g protein / 11 g total fat / 1.5 g saturated fat / 131 mg sodium

GINGER-SPIKED PEACH FIZZ

If you are running for two or have a big race coming up, this refreshing drink will make you feel like you're sipping a summer cocktail.

MAKES 2 SERVINGS // TOTAL TIME: 5 MINUTES

1 piece (½") fresh ginger, peeled

2 bottles (12 ounces each) peach-flavored seltzer water

Grate the ginger into 2 tall glasses and add the seltzer. Serve immediately.

NUTRITION PER SERVING 0 calories / 0 g carbohydrates / 0 g fiber / 0 g sugars / 0 g protein / 0 g total fat / 0 g saturated fat / 0 mg sodium

ICED SPICED COCOA LATTE

Save your money (and your rush-hour wait) by making your own iced mocha, perfect after a summer run. Have it before your run, too, if it doesn't bother your stomach.

MAKES 6 SERVINGS // TOTAL TIME: 10 MINUTES, PLUS CHILLING TIME

3   cups water
5   tablespoons freshly ground coffee
¼   teaspoon ground cinnamon
2   tablespoons sugar
1   tablespoon unsweetened cocoa powder
3   cups 1% milk
6   cinnamon sticks

Place the water in a coffeemaker. In a small bowl, mix the coffee and cinnamon and use to brew 1 pot of coffee. Stir in the sugar and cocoa powder, and chill until cold.

Pour equal amounts of coffee into 6 glasses filled with ice. Mix well and top each off with ½ cup milk.

Garnish with the cinnamon sticks.

NUTRITION PER SERVING   71 calories / 11 g carbohydrates / 0 g fiber / 10 g sugars / 4 g protein / 1 g total fat / 1 g saturated fat / 56 mg sodium

HONEYDEW LIME COOLER

Make your own summer drink, and you'll know exactly how many calories and how much sugar are in it. Honeydew is refreshing and a good source of vitamin C. It even has a little bit of iron in it.

MAKES 4 SERVINGS // TOTAL TIME: 10 MINUTES

2 **cups cubed peeled honeydew**
1 **cup water**
Juice of 1 lime
Seltzer, chilled
Agave, to taste (optional)
Fresh mint sprigs, for garnish
4 **strawberries, for garnish**
1 **lime, sliced, for garnish**

In a blender or food processor, combine the honeydew, water, and lime juice. Puree until smooth. Pour the mixture through a fine-mesh strainer, pushing the pulp down with a spoon to release more liquid.

Divide the liquid among 4 glasses and top each one off with seltzer. Sweeten with agave, if desired. Garnish each glass with mint, a strawberry, and a lime slice.

NUTRITION PER SERVING 33 calories / 9 g carbohydrates / 1 g fiber / 7 g sugars / 1 g protein / 0 g total fat / 0 g saturated fat / 17 mg sodium

MEXICAN COFFEE

Literally spice up your morning roast by adding a Mexican twist. Traditionally brewed with darkly roasted beans similar to Viennese roast, *café de olla* ("coffee from the pot") has a spicy kick. To warm the coffee mugs, fill them with hot tap water and let stand for a few minutes. (Be sure to dump the water before adding the coffee!)

MAKES 2 SERVINGS // TOTAL TIME: 15 MINUTES

3	tablespoons coarsely ground French roast or other dark-roast coffee
2	tablespoons muscovado or dark brown sugar
2	cinnamon sticks
2	whole cloves
2	cups water

In a small saucepan, combine the coffee, sugar, cinnamon sticks, cloves, and water. Bring to a boil over high heat, stirring frequently. Reduce the heat to medium-low, cover, and simmer for 10 minutes. Strain into 2 warmed coffee mugs and serve hot.

NUTRITION PER SERVING   55 calories / 14 g carbohydrates / 0 g fiber / 13 g sugars / 0 g protein / 0 g total fat / 0 g saturated fat / 9 mg sodium

CARDAMOM-GINGER CHAI TEA

Black tea can have up to 70 milligrams of caffeine per cup, which can help with alertness but is still less than a cup of coffee (95 to 200 milligrams). If you need to sweeten your tea, maple syrup and honey are natural sugars, and unlike table sugar, they have vitamins and minerals.

MAKES 2 SERVINGS // TOTAL TIME: 10 MINUTES

1½ cups water

4   whole green cardamom pods, smashed

2   thin slices (1" diameter) fresh ginger

1   piece (1") cinnamon stick

1   whole clove

1½ cups 1% milk or unsweetened milk alternative

1½ teaspoons loose-leaf black tea

1   teaspoon vanilla extract

1   teaspoon pure maple syrup or honey (optional)

In a small saucepan, combine the water, cardamom, ginger, cinnamon stick, and clove. Bring the mixture to a boil. Reduce the heat to low and simmer for 3 minutes, or until fragrant.

Add the milk, tea leaves, and vanilla and simmer for 1 minute. Turn off the heat and let steep for 2 minutes.

Strain into 2 cups through a fine-mesh sieve (discard the tea leaves and spices). If desired, sweeten each with ½ teaspoon maple syrup or honey.

NUTRITION PER SERVING

84 calories / 10 g carbohydrates / 0 g fiber / 9 g sugars / 6 g protein / 2 g total fat / 1.5 g saturated fat / 81 mg sodium

HOT GINGERED CIDER WITH LADY APPLES

You know what they say about an apple a day ... This fall favorite is high in quercetin, which may keep blood sugar stable. Research has also found that an apple in the morning can help jump-start your run just like a cup of coffee. You can prepare this cider up to 6 hours before serving. The longer it steeps, the more the clove and ginger flavors will be enhanced.

MAKES 10 SERVINGS // TOTAL TIME: 20 MINUTES

20 whole cloves, or more to taste

10 Lady apples, or other small apples

2 quarts fresh apple cider

1 piece (3") fresh ginger, peeled and roughly chopped

Push 2 cloves into each apple.

In a Dutch oven or soup pot, combine the cider, ginger, and apples, and bring to a boil over high heat. Reduce to a simmer and cook, partially covered, for 10 to 15 minutes, or until heated through.

Strain the ginger from the cider and serve the cider hot with a clove-pierced apple in each mug.

NUTRITION PER SERVING

159 calories / 41 g carbohydrates / 3 g fiber / 33 g sugars / 0 g protein / 0 g total fat / 0 g saturated fat / 21 mg sodium

PASSION FRUIT, PINEAPPLE, AND MINT COOLER

This recipe was inspired by runners in tropical climates who use mint and fruits to make refreshing drinks. Pour yourself a glass after a hot run to cool off.

MAKES 4 SERVINGS // TOTAL TIME: 10 MINUTES

2 tablespoons chopped fresh mint leaves

2 tablespoons sugar

3 ripe passion fruits, or ½ cup thawed frozen passion fruit pulp

½ cup unsweetened pineapple juice

4 cups cold water

1 cup diced fresh pineapple (optional)

In a large pitcher, combine the mint and sugar. Using the handle of a large wooden spoon, muddle the mint into the sugar until the sugar looks like wet sand.

If using fresh passion fruits, cut the fruit in half and scoop the pulp into a blender. Add ¼ cup water and pulse to help the pulp release from the seeds. Pass through a fine-mesh sieve, pressing down to release all the juice. Discard the seeds.

Add the passion fruit pulp (fresh or frozen) to the pitcher along with the pineapple juice, cold water, and diced pineapple, if using. Serve over ice.

NUTRITION PER SERVING 60 calories / 15 g carbohydrates / 0 g fiber / 14 g sugars / 0 g protein / 0 g total fat / 0 g saturated fat / 12 mg sodium

3
SNACKS

TRAIL MIXES

OLD-FASHIONED

Peanuts, raisins,
chocolate chips, pretzels

SWEET 'N' SALTY

Peanuts, walnuts, cranberries,
sunflower seeds, candied ginger,
chocolate chips, pinch of sea salt

TROPICAL VACATION

Macadamia nuts, Brazil nuts,
coconut flakes, dried mango, dried
pineapple, banana chips

PUMPKIN SPICE

Pumpkin seeds, popcorn,
pistachios, candied ginger,
granola, dash of cinnamon and
nutmeg

GO NUTS

Peanuts, cashews, almonds,
Brazil nuts, walnuts, pecans,
pistachios, macadamia nuts

THE KICK

Pistachios, wasabi peas,
hemp seeds, dried mango

SWEET TOOTH

Hazelnuts, chocolate chips,
dried cranberries, granola,
coconut flakes

WAKE ME UP

Chocolate-covered coffee/
espresso beans, cashews,
almonds, dried apricots, rice cereal

FIGHT THE WALL

Walnuts, peanuts, dried cherries,
banana chips, chocolate-covered
coffee/espresso beans, pretzels

NUTTER BUTTER

Vegan marshmallows, peanuts,
chocolate chips, banana chips

ALLERGIES BE GONE

Raisins, dried cranberries, rice
cereal, popcorn

ANTIOXIDANT POWERHOUSE

Dried blueberries, dried cherries,
dried cranberries, almonds,
pistachios, walnuts, dash of cinnamon

BREAKFAST TO GO

Banana chips, dried cranberries, dried apricots, almonds, pecans, granola

COMING OUT OF THE CAJUN

Wasabi peas, almonds, peanuts, sunflower seeds, pumpkin seeds, pinch of Cajun seasoning

PROTEIN POWER

Peanuts, cashews, almonds, dates, dried apricots, pumpkin seeds, chocolate chips

RECOVERY MIX

Peanuts, Brazil nuts, banana chips, flaxseeds, candied ginger, granola

ASIAN FUSION

Roasted edamame, wasabi peas, candied ginger, sesame seeds, dried mango

MIDRUN FUEL

Raisins, banana chips, dried apricots, pretzels

PB&J

Peanuts, dried strawberries, raisins, rice cereal

EARTHY CRUNCHY

Almonds, walnuts, dried apricots, dates, flaxseeds, hemp seeds, chocolate chips

PRERACE MOVIE NIGHT

Popcorn, pistachios, dried cherries, chocolate chips

TURKEY TROT MIX

Pecans, pumpkin seeds, granola, dried cranberries, pinch of nutmeg and cinnamon

S'MORE MILES

Pretzels, vegan marshmallows, chocolate chips

COCONUT-ALMOND ENERGY BARS

Adapted from The Baker in New Paltz, New York, these energy-packed bars are made with oats, dates, honey (for quick fuel), and nuts and seeds (for satiety and protein). Instead of heading to the office vending machine when hunger strikes, try one of these for an afternoon pick-me-up.

MAKES 20 SERVINGS // TOTAL TIME: 25 MINUTES

2 cups old-fashioned rolled oats
1 cup unsweetened shredded coconut
½ cup whole raw almonds
½ cup whole raw cashews or peanuts
½ cup sesame seeds
½ cup raw sunflower seeds
½ cup chopped dates or raisins
1½ cups tahini or natural peanut butter
1 cup honey (you'll need an entire 16-ounce bottle)
1 teaspoon vanilla extract

Preheat the oven to 350°F. Generously coat a 15" × 10" baking sheet with cooking spray.

In a large bowl, combine the oats, coconut, almonds, cashews or peanuts, sesame seeds, sunflower seeds, and dates or raisins.

In a microwaveable bowl, combine the tahini or peanut butter and the honey. Microwave on high power for 1 minute. Add the vanilla and mix well. Add to the oat mixture. Stir until well combined.

Pour the mixture onto the baking sheet and, with wet hands, pat into a rectangle about 1" high (your rectangle will be about 12" × 10"). Bake for 15 minutes, or until the edges of the bars turn golden brown. Do not overbake. Slice into 20 bars before cooling. The bars will still feel tacky in the center but will firm up as they cool.

NUTRITION PER SERVING (1 BAR)

311 calories / 30 g carbohydrates / 5 g fiber / 18 g sugars / 8 g protein / 20 g total fat / 5 g saturated fat / 26 mg sodium

CRUNCHY CURRY PEAS

More filling and nutritious than a bag of potato chips, peas are high in fiber. Curry powder uses turmeric, which has been shown to have anti-inflammatory benefits after hard exercise.

MAKES 4 SERVINGS // TOTAL TIME: 25 MINUTES, PLUS 4 HOURS SOAK TIME

⅔ **cup yellow split peas**

¼ **cup canola oil**

2 **teaspoons curry powder**

½ **teaspoon salt**

In a bowl, soak the split peas in water for 4 hours. Drain and pat dry.

In a skillet over low-medium heat, heat the oil. Add the peas and cook, stirring often, for 15 minutes, or until golden. Transfer to a paper towel–lined plate.

Toss with the curry powder and salt.

NUTRITION PER SERVING

144 calories / 20 g carbohydrates / 10 g fiber / 1 g sugars / 7 g protein / 4 g total fat / 0 g saturated fat / 292 mg sodium

CHOCOLATE CHIP TRAIL MIX BALLS

Runners love trail mix, and it's no wonder: It's high in fiber, good-for-you fat, and natural sugar from dried fruit, and it's portable. These trail mix balls take the portability to another level, since you can just pop them in your mouth for quick energy. Have a couple an hour or so before a run; they're also perfect for a grab-and-go breakfast. To make this dish vegan, use agave syrup instead of honey.

MAKES 12 SERVINGS // TOTAL TIME: 15 MINUTES

½   **cup almond butter**
⅓   **cup agave syrup or honey**
1½ **cups old-fashioned rolled oats**
¼   **cup hulled pumpkin seeds**
¼   **cup dark chocolate mini chips**
¼   **cup chopped dried tart cherries**
¼   **cup sliced almonds**
½   **cup toasted wheat germ**

In a bowl, with an electric mixer on low speed, mix together the almond butter and agave syrup or honey for 2 minutes, or until smooth and well combined.

With the mixer still on low, gradually add the oats until well combined, followed by the pumpkin seeds. Add the chocolate chips, cherries, and almonds. Mix for 1 minute, or until just combined.

Line a baking sheet with waxed paper. Place the wheat germ in a shallow bowl. For each ball, use a tablespoon to take a heaping scoop of the mixture and, with your hands, gently roll into a ball. Roll in the wheat germ and set on the baking sheet.

You can eat the trail mix balls immediately, or transfer any uneaten ones, still on the baking sheet, to the refrigerator for 2 hours, or until set. Transfer the chilled balls to a plastic freezer bag and store in the fridge for up to 2 weeks.

NUTRITION PER SERVING (2 BALLS)

209 calories / 24 g carbohydrates / 5 g fiber / 11 g sugars / 7 g protein / 11 g total fat / 2 g saturated fat / 31 mg sodium

SPINACH-TOFU PUFFS

Adding tofu to a cheesy spinach puff is a good way to sneak in extra protein. These indulgent balls, perfect for a get-together, can be prepared in advance and frozen before baking. When ready to use, bake an extra 10 minutes.

MAKES 8 SERVINGS // TOTAL TIME: 30 MINUTES

1   package (10 ounces) frozen spinach, thawed and squeezed dry

1½ cups whole grain cracker crumbs or dried bread crumbs

1   pound firm tofu, mashed

½   cup finely chopped Vidalia onion

3   large eggs, lightly beaten

⅓   cup unsalted butter, melted

¼   cup grated Parmesan cheese

1   teaspoon minced garlic

½   teaspoon salt

½   teaspoon ground black pepper

¼   teaspoon dried thyme

Preheat the oven to 325°F. Grease a baking sheet.

In a large bowl, combine the spinach, cracker crumbs or bread crumbs, tofu, onion, eggs, butter, cheese, garlic, salt, pepper, and thyme and mix well.

Shape into 1" balls and place on the baking sheet. Bake for 15 to 20 minutes, or until puffed and cooked through.

NUTRITION PER SERVING

283 calories / 20 g carbohydrates / 3 g fiber / 2 g sugars / 16 g protein / 16 g total fat / 7 g saturated fat / 394 mg sodium

MAPLE PEPITAS

Pumpkin seeds (*pepitas* in Spanish) are a good source of vitamin E and healthy fat. Eat these pepitas as-is or toss into trail mix for a boost of nutrition.

MAKES 8 SERVINGS // TOTAL TIME: 15 MINUTES

2   **cups hulled pumpkin seeds**
2   **tablespoons maple syrup**
1½ **teaspoons coarse salt**
½   **teaspoon paprika or cayenne pepper**

Preheat the oven to 425°F. Line a baking sheet with parchment paper.

In a bowl, combine the pumpkin seeds, maple syrup, salt, and paprika or cayenne pepper, and toss well.

Spread the mixture out in a single layer on the baking sheet. Bake for 10 to 15 minutes, or until the seeds are golden brown and aromatic. Store in an airtight container.

NUTRITION PER SERVING (¼ CUP)

194 calories / 7 g carbohydrates / 2 g fiber / 4 g sugars / 10 g protein / 16 g total fat / 3 g saturated fat / 367 mg sodium

PUMPKIN PIE TRAIL MIX POPCORN

Popcorn, when it's not soaked in butter, is an excellent snack that's packed with whole grains. Toss in fixins like pumpkin seeds and coconut, and you've added heart-healthy fat that will help you feel full during movie night.

MAKES 1 SERVING // TOTAL TIME: 5 MINUTES

1   cup air-popped popcorn

2   tablespoons hulled pumpkin seeds

1   tablespoon unsweetened coconut

    Pinch of pumpkin pie spice and/or ground cinnamon

In a medium bowl, toss the popcorn with the pumpkin seeds, coconut, and pumpkin pie spice and/or cinnamon.

NUTRITION PER SERVING

156 calories / 10 g carbohydrates / 3 g fiber / 1 g sugars / 6 g protein / 11 g total fat / 4.5 g saturated fat / 5 mg sodium

CHILI-LIME KALE CHIPS

Believe the hype when it comes to kale chips. A little bit of spice transforms this leafy green superfood, packed with folate and potassium, into a nutrient-packed snack that puts an ordinary potato chip to shame.

MAKES 2 SERVINGS // TOTAL TIME: 25 MINUTES

6	cups roughly chopped kale leaves (tough ribs removed)
1	tablespoon grapeseed oil
⅛	teaspoon fine sea salt (or more to taste)
⅛	teaspoon chili powder (or more to taste)
1	teaspoon grated lime zest (or more to taste)

Preheat the oven to 350°F. Lightly oil a baking sheet or line with parchment paper.

Place the kale in a large bowl. Drizzle with the oil and sprinkle with the salt. Use your hands to massage the oil and salt into the kale until evenly coated.

Arrange the kale in a single layer on the baking sheet. Bake for 10 minutes. Remove the baking sheet from the oven and, using tongs, carefully turn the kale chips over. Return the baking sheet to the oven and bake for 5 minutes, or until crispy.

Sprinkle with the chili powder and lime zest. If desired, season with more salt and chili powder to taste. Serve immediately.

NUTRITION PER SERVING

159 calories / 18 g carbohydrates / 4 g fiber / 0 g sugars / 9 g protein / 9 g total fat / 1 g saturated fat / 175 mg sodium

ZUCCHINI COINS

Pair these lightly sautéed coins with a dollop of Greek yogurt for a prerun snack or an afternoon nibble.

MAKES 4 SERVINGS // TOTAL TIME: 15 MINUTES

1   pound zucchini, sliced into rounds
1   tablespoon olive oil
1   tablespoon chopped fresh rosemary
¼   teaspoon salt
¼   teaspoon ground black pepper

Preheat the broiler with a rack 6" from the heat source. Line a baking sheet with foil and coat with cooking spray.

In a bowl, toss the zucchini rounds with the oil, rosemary, salt, and pepper. Arrange in an even layer on the baking sheet. Broil, turning once, for 8 minutes, or until golden.

NUTRITION PER SERVING

50 calories / 4 g carbohydrates / 1 g fiber / 3 g sugars / 1 g protein / 4 g total fat / 0.5 g saturated fat / 155 mg sodium

SOUTH-OF-THE-BORDER SNACK MIX

Toss a small bagful of this snack mix into your gym bag for a preworkout snack. Roasted soy nuts are a good source of plant protein and are a tasty substitute if you have a nut allergy (or just need a break from nuts!).

MAKES 16 SERVINGS // TOTAL TIME: 2 HOURS 5 MINUTES

3   tablespoons canola oil
1   tablespoon ground cumin
1   teaspoon grated lime zest
1   tablespoon fresh lime juice
8   cups hexagonal multigrain cereal
6   to 8 cups air-popped popcorn, lightly salted
¼   cup roasted soy nuts

In a measuring cup, whisk together the oil, cumin, lime zest, and lime juice.

In a 4- or 5-quart slow cooker, combine the cereal, popcorn, and nuts. Drizzle with the oil mixture. Toss to coat. Cover and cook on low for 2 hours, tossing once. (Alternatively, preheat the oven to 400°F. Spread the cereal, popcorn, and nuts evenly on a baking sheet and bake for 10 minutes, or until the nuts are toasted. Drizzle with the oil mixture and toss to coat.)

NUTRITION PER SERVING

106 calories / 17 g carbohydrates / 1 g fiber / 2 g sugars / 2 g protein / 3 g total fat / 0.5 g saturated fat / 142 mg sodium

TROPICAL FRUIT BARS

Bring snacking to a whole new level with these homemade fruit bars, packed with whole grains and natural sugar. Leave a few in your desk for an afternoon snack or toss one in your fuel belt for a midrun carb hit.

MAKES 12 SERVINGS // TOTAL TIME: 50 MINUTES

- 1 **cup pitted dates, finely chopped**
- ¾ **cup well-drained juice-packed crushed pineapple, juice reserved**
- 1½ **cups whole wheat flour**
- 1 **cup old-fashioned rolled oats**
- ½ **cup flaked coconut**
- ¼ **cup date sugar**
- 1 **teaspoon coarse salt**
- ¼ **teaspoon baking soda**
- ½ **cup (1 stick) butter, cut into tablespoons**
- 1 **large egg, beaten**

In a 1-quart saucepan, combine the dates, pineapple, and ¼ cup of the reserved pineapple juice. Bring to a boil, reduce to a simmer, and cook, stirring occasionally, for 5 minutes, or until the mixture has thickened. Set aside.

Preheat the oven to 375°F. Butter an 8" × 8" baking pan.

In a food processor, combine the flour, oats, coconut, date sugar, salt, and baking soda and pulse to blend. Add the butter and pulse until the mixture resembles coarse crumbs. Press half of the crumb mixture firmly onto the bottom of the baking pan. Spread the pineapple-date mixture on top. Stir the egg into the remaining crumb mixture and spread evenly over the filling.

Bake for 25 to 30 minutes, or until lightly browned. Cool in the pan on a wire rack. Cut into 12 bars.

| **NUTRITION PER SERVING (1 BAR)** | 223 calories / 32 g carbohydrates / 4 g fiber / 15 g sugars / 4 g protein / 10 g total fat / 6 g saturated fat / 204 mg sodium |

FLAX AND OAT CRACKERS

Oats and flax are a good source of fiber, which supports digestion and heart health. Pair these homemade crackers with a fruit spread and cheese for a postrun snack.

MAKES 12 SERVINGS // TOTAL TIME: 45 MINUTES

¾ **cup old-fashioned rolled oats**

1 **cup white whole wheat flour (milled from white wheat grains)**

½ **cup oat bran**

½ **teaspoon salt**

¼ **cup + 2 tablespoons vegetable oil**

1 **tablespoon honey**

½ **cup water**

2 **tablespoons golden flaxseeds**

Preheat the oven to 350°F. Lightly oil a large baking sheet.

In a spice mill, coffee mill, or mini food processor, grind the oats to a fine meal.

In a medium bowl, whisk together the oat meal, flour, oat bran, and salt. In a large bowl, blend the oil and honey together. Stir in the flour mixture and water and mix just until the dough is smooth.

Press or roll the dough to a ⅛" thickness right on the baking sheet. Sprinkle with the flaxseeds and press them lightly into the dough so they adhere. With a sharp knife, cut the dough into 2" squares. Bake for 12 to 15 minutes, or until lightly golden. Cool for 5 minutes, then remove from the pan.

NUTRITION PER SERVING

131 calories / 15 g carbohydrates / 2 g fiber / 2 g sugars / 3 g protein / 8 g total fat / 1 g saturated fat / 98 mg sodium

SWEET POTATO–COCONUT FRITTERS

These baked fritters are packed with flavor, vitamin A, and, thanks to the sweet potato and coconut, medium-chain fatty acids, which may boost your body's metabolism. Serve with a scoop of Greek yogurt for protein and calcium.

MAKES 12 SERVINGS // TOTAL TIME: 45 MINUTES

2	sweet potatoes (6 ounces each), peeled and cut into chunks
1	teaspoon water
1	egg yolk
1	tablespoon cornmeal
2	cloves garlic, minced
1	teaspoon minced fresh ginger
½	teaspoon baking powder
⅛	teaspoon salt
3	tablespoons unsweetened flaked coconut

Preheat the oven to 350°F. Coat a nonstick baking sheet with cooking spray.

Place the sweet potatoes on a microwaveable plate with the water. Cover with microwave-safe plastic wrap and microwave on high power for 6 minutes, or until soft. Let stand for 3 minutes. Mash with a fork.

In a food processor, combine the sweet potatoes, egg yolk, cornmeal, garlic, ginger, baking powder, and salt. Pulse about 6 times, scraping down the sides of the container as needed, until a coarse puree forms.

Drop the batter onto the baking sheet in 24 equal dollops. Top each with some of the coconut, pressing gently to adhere. Bake for 15 minutes, or until the coconut starts to brown. Serve warm or at room temperature.

NUTRITION PER SERVING (2 FRITTERS)
39 calories / 6 g carbohydrates / 1 g fiber / 1 g sugars / 1 g protein / 1 g total fat / 1 g saturated fat / 55 mg sodium

BEE POLLEN POPCORN

If you do it right (as in, avoid the movie theater popcorn, which can be soaked in salt and butter), popcorn can be a healthy, nutritious, filling snack that you can eat without guilt. Customize the whole grain (yes, it is a whole grain!) by topping it with your favorite spices. The coconut oil in this recipe makes for a creamy, flavorful movie-night snack. Topped with bee pollen, it has a hint of sweetness without the extra calories (and may help improve those springtime allergies—good news if you're running an April or May marathon!).

MAKES 6 SERVINGS // TOTAL TIME: 10 MINUTES

2   tablespoons coconut oil
½   cup unpopped popcorn kernels
    Salt and ground black pepper, to taste
¼   cup bee pollen, plus more to taste

In a large saucepan with a lid, melt the coconut oil over medium heat. Add 3 or 4 kernels and cover. When the tester kernels pop, add the remaining kernels and cover, leaving a small opening to let steam escape.

Shake the pan back and forth during the heavy popping, about 3 minutes. When the popping slows down to no pops for 5 seconds, remove the pan from the heat and give it a final shake.

Pour the popcorn into a large bowl and season to taste with salt and pepper. Toss with the bee pollen, adding more if desired.

NUTRITION PER SERVING   128 calories / 16 g carbohydrates / 3 g fiber / 0 g sugars / 4 g protein / 6 g total fat / 4 g saturated fat / 321 mg sodium

COCONUT-CURRY SNACK MIX

Created by professional (twin!) triathletes, this snack is a go-to for race travel. "We pack it in zip-top bags and toss it in our carry-on bags or in the front console of the car," the Wassner twins say. Bulk it up with pretzels or toasted pumpkin seeds.

MAKES 8 SERVINGS // TOTAL TIME: 20 MINUTES, PLUS COOLING TIME

- 3 cups (8 ounces) unsweetened flaked coconut
- ½ cup sliced almonds
- ¼ cup maple syrup
- 1 tablespoon sesame seeds
- ½ to ¾ teaspoon curry powder
   Pinch of flaky sea salt

Preheat the oven to 325°F. Line a large rimmed baking sheet with parchment paper.

In a large bowl, gently fold the coconut, almonds, maple syrup, sesame seeds, and curry powder until combined and completely coated. Spread the mixture evenly on the baking sheet. Sprinkle with sea salt.

Bake for 10 minutes, rotating the pan halfway through, or until the coconut and almonds are golden brown. Keep careful watch because the coconut can burn easily. Pull the pan out of the oven if it looks like the flakes are starting to get too dark.

Cool completely before storing in an airtight container.

NUTRITION PER SERVING

307 calories / 16 g carbohydrates / 5 g fiber / 9 g sugars / 4 g protein / 26 g total fat / 19 g saturated fat / 48 mg sodium

CARROT HUMMUS

A perfect snack or appetizer, this vibrant bright orange hummus promises to be a hit. It's easy to prepare and a great alternative to a traditional chickpea-based hummus. You'll find it's easy to finish a whole bowl of this light, healthy, and flavorful hummus with some pita chips and vegetables (without the guilt).

MAKES 8 SERVINGS // TOTAL TIME: 40 MINUTES

1½ pounds carrots, trimmed, peeled, and halved crosswise

1   teaspoon + ¼ cup olive oil

1   teaspoon kosher salt, plus more to taste

2   tablespoons tahini, plus more to taste

1   tablespoon red wine vinegar, plus more to taste

1   teaspoon ground cumin, plus more to taste

Preheat the oven to 400°F. Line a large rimmed baking sheet with parchment paper.

Place the carrots on the baking sheet. Drizzle with 1 teaspoon of the oil and sprinkle with the salt. Toss to coat the carrots. Roast for 25 minutes, or until the carrots are starting to caramelize.

Let the carrots cool for 5 to 10 minutes. Place the roasted carrots in a food processor. Add the remaining ¼ cup oil, the tahini, vinegar, and cumin. Blend for 1 to 2 minutes, or until thick and smooth. Season with more salt, cumin, vinegar, and/or tahini as desired.

NUTRITION PER SERVING

123 calories / 9 g carbohydrates / 3 g fiber / 4 g sugars / 2 g protein / 10 g total fat / 1 g saturated fat / 301 mg sodium

GREEN CHILE GUACAMOLE

Everyone knows that no runner gathering is complete without guacamole. Throw together this recipe before your teammates come over for a heart-healthy snack packed with vitamin C, thanks to avocados. Serve with tortilla chips for a traditional dip, or up your veggie intake with carrot, celery, and bell pepper sticks. (As elite runner and recipe developer Matt Llano says, "You really just need a vehicle for the guac, right?")

MAKES 12 SERVINGS // TOTAL TIME: 5 MINUTES, PLUS 1 HOUR RESTING TIME

4   **or 5 ripe avocados**
    Juice of 1 lime
½   **teaspoon kosher salt**
1   **can (10 ounces) diced tomatoes and green chilies, drained**
¼   **cup finely chopped red onion**
¼   **cup chopped fresh cilantro**
¼   **to 1 jalapeño chile pepper, chopped**
¼   **teaspoon ground black pepper**

Halve the avocados and remove the pits. Scoop the flesh out into a large bowl. Add the lime juice and salt and mash with a fork until you reach your desired guacamole consistency.

Stir in the tomatoes and chilies, onion, cilantro, jalapeño pepper, and black pepper. For best results, cover and let the flavors meld in the refrigerator for 1 to 2 hours before serving.

NUTRITION PER SERVING (¼ CUP)

114 calories / 7 g carbohydrates / 5 g fiber / 1 g sugars / 2 g protein / 10 g total fat / 1.5 g saturated fat / 180 mg sodium

CHIPOTLE–SWEET POTATO HUMMUS

Yes, you can carb-load on hummus—when it's packed with sweet potatoes, that is. Spice up your everyday dip with a kick of chipotle that will rev your metabolism, and tahini, an excellent source of copper, which helps your body absorb iron. Serve with veggies, a sliced baguette, or whole grain chips.

MAKES 12 SERVINGS // TOTAL TIME: 10 MINUTES

¼ cup tahini

3 tablespoons fresh lemon juice

3 cloves garlic, coarsely chopped

1 teaspoon kosher salt

1 can (15 ounces) chickpeas, rinsed and drained

1 to 2 tablespoons diced chipotle peppers in adobo sauce

2 tablespoons + 1 teaspoon extra-virgin olive oil, divided

1 can (15 ounces) sweet potato puree

1 teaspoon ground cumin

¾ teaspoon smoked paprika, divided

2 tablespoons roasted salted hulled pumpkin seeds

In a food processor, combine the tahini, lemon juice, garlic, and salt. Pulse until smooth. Add the chickpeas and chipotle peppers and pulse to combine. With the food processor running, drizzle in 2 tablespoons of the oil until a slightly runny paste forms. Add the sweet potato puree, cumin, and ½ teaspoon of the paprika and process for 1 minute, or until combined and smooth.

Transfer the hummus to a serving bowl. Top with the remaining 1 teaspoon oil, ¼ teaspoon paprika, and the pumpkin seeds.

NUTRITION PER SERVING (¼ CUP)

129 calories / 15 g carbohydrates / 3 g fiber / 3 g sugars / 4 g protein / 7 g total fat / 1 g saturated fat / 180 mg sodium

BANANA FROZEN "YOGURT"

No, this isn't a true substitute for ice cream. But it *is* a creamy, refreshing snack that has a similar consistency to the real thing, thanks to the pectin found in bananas. Mix with nut butter for a boost of protein and flavor.

MAKES 1 SERVING // TOTAL TIME: 10 MINUTES, PLUS FREEZING TIME

1   cup frozen peeled banana chunks
1   tablespoon nut butter (optional)

In a food processor, blend the banana. The banana will start to crumble. Scrape the sides and keep blending for 5 minutes, or until the texture starts to become creamy. Add the nut butter, if using.

Blend until the consistency is like soft-serve ice cream. Eat immediately for soft serve or freeze until stiffer for a traditional ice cream texture.

NUTRITION PER SERVING

WITHOUT NUT BUTTER: 105 calories / 27 g carbohydrates / 3 g fiber / 14 g sugars / 1 g protein / 0 g total fat / 0 g saturated fat / 1 mg sodium
WITH NUT BUTTER: 201 calories / 30 g carbohydrates / 5 g fiber / 15 g sugars / 5 g protein / 9 g total fat / 1 g saturated fat / 37 mg sodium

4
SIDE DISHES

POTATO LATKES

For runners, pasta tends to get all the carb-load hype. But potatoes are an excellent source of carbohydrates to fuel those long miles. Try these potato pancakes—or latkes, as they were called by their Jewish creators—and top with one of our favorite sauces.

MAKES 4 SERVINGS // TOTAL TIME: 50 MINUTES

- **1** **pound potatoes (russet, gold, or purple), scrubbed**
- **1** **medium onion, halved**
- **1** **teaspoon kosher salt, plus more to taste**
- **1** **large egg, lightly beaten**
- **½** **cup all-purpose flour**
- **6** **to 8 tablespoons canola or olive oil, for frying**

Using a food processor or box grater, grate the potatoes and the onion. Place in a colander lined with a clean kitchen towel or cheesecloth and sprinkle with the salt. Let stand for 30 minutes.

Using the towel or cheesecloth, squeeze as much liquid as possible from the potatoes and onion. Place the drained mixture in a large bowl.

Add the egg and flour to the potato mixture and stir to combine thoroughly.

In a large skillet over medium-high heat, heat the oil until it is shimmering. Drop about ¼ cup of the potato mixture per latke into the hot oil and flatten into a patty about ¼" thick. Cook for 4 minutes, turning once, or until golden. Remove to a paper towel–lined plate and sprinkle with salt to taste. Repeat with the remaining potato mixture, frying several at once but not crowding the pan.

Serve warm or at room temperature with Caramelized Shallots (page 105) or Apple-Pear Sauce (page 106).

NUTRITION PER SERVING (2 LATKES)

356 calories / 35 g carbohydrates / 2 g fiber / 2 g sugars / 6 g protein / 22 g total fat / 2 g saturated fat / 601 mg sodium

CARROT-PARSNIP LATKES

For a tasty nutrient boost to your traditional potato latke (see page 102), use carrots and parsnips. They'll add a little sweetness, fiber, and vitamin C.

MAKES 4 SERVINGS // TOTAL TIME: 50 MINUTES

2 medium carrots (4 ounces total), peeled

1 medium parsnip (4 ounces), peeled

½ pound potatoes (russet, gold, or purple), scrubbed

1 medium onion, halved

1 teaspoon kosher salt, plus more to taste

1 large egg, lightly beaten

½ cup all-purpose flour

6 to 8 tablespoons canola or olive oil, for frying

Using a food processor or box grater, grate the carrots, parsnip, potatoes, and onion. Place the grated vegetables in a colander lined with a clean kitchen towel or cheesecloth and sprinkle with the salt. Let stand for 30 minutes.

Using the towel or cheesecloth, squeeze as much liquid as possible from the vegetables. Place the drained mixture in a large bowl.

Add the egg and flour to the vegetable mixture and stir to combine thoroughly.

In a large skillet over medium-high heat, heat the oil until it is shimmering. Drop about ¼ cup of the vegetable mixture per latke into the hot oil and flatten into a patty about ¼" thick. Cook for 4 minutes, turning once, or until golden. Remove to a paper towel–lined plate and sprinkle with salt to taste. Repeat with the remaining vegetable mixture, frying several at once but not crowding the pan.

Serve warm or at room temperature with Caramelized Shallots (opposite) or Apple-Pear Sauce (page 106).

NUTRITION PER SERVING (2 LATKES)

343 calories / 32 g carbohydrates / 4 g fiber / 4 g sugars / 5 g protein / 23 g total fat / 2 g saturated fat / 623 mg sodium

CARAMELIZED SHALLOTS

Unlike onions, shallots have a sweet and mild flavor, with a hint of garlic. Caramelize them and you've got a sweet topper, perfect for any potato latke.

MAKES 4 SERVINGS // TOTAL TIME: 30 MINUTES

1   tablespoon olive oil
6   shallots, sliced
½   teaspoon kosher salt

In a medium skillet over medium-low heat, warm the oil. Add the shallots and salt and stir to coat in the oil. Cook, stirring often, for 20 to 25 minutes, or until soft and browned. If the shallots start to stick or burn, add a splash of water to the skillet.

NUTRITION PER SERVING (2 TABLESPOONS)

110 calories / 20 g carbohydrates / 0 g fiber / 4 g sugars / 4 g protein / 3 g total fat / 0.5 g saturated fat / 192 mg sodium

SIDE DISHES

APPLE-PEAR SAUCE

This sauce is a welcome twist on the traditional applesauce used to top potato latkes. It also works great as a mix-in for your postrun oatmeal.

MAKES 4 SERVINGS // TOTAL TIME: 25 MINUTES

1   apple, peeled, cored, and chopped
1   pear, peeled, cored, and chopped
1   teaspoon honey or maple syrup
½   teaspoon ground cinnamon
2   tablespoons water
    Pinch of salt

In a medium saucepan over medium-low heat, combine the apple, pear, honey or maple syrup, cinnamon, and water. Stir, cover, and cook, stirring occasionally, for 15 to 20 minutes, or until the fruit is very soft and broken down. If desired, run a potato masher through the mixture. Stir in the salt, remove from the heat, and cool to room temperature.

PRO TIP

To make this topping vegan, use maple syrup instead of honey.

NUTRITION PER SERVING (¼ CUP)

55 calories / 15 g carbohydrates / 3 g fiber / 11 g sugars / 0 g protein / 0 g total fat / 0 g saturated fat / 38 mg sodium

ROASTED SWEET POTATO WEDGES

"I usually make potatoes at least once a week," says plant-based ultrarunner Scott Jurek. "I look for different types—purple potatoes, Yukon Golds, sweet potatoes." Potatoes are an excellent source of carbohydrates, fiber (when you eat the skin!), potassium, and vitamin C. Sweet potatoes are also high in vitamin A.

MAKES 4 SERVINGS // TOTAL TIME: 25 MINUTES

4   sweet potatoes, sliced lengthwise into wedges
1   tablespoon extra-virgin olive oil
1   teaspoon salt
1   teaspoon paprika
1   teaspoon crushed dried rosemary

Preheat the oven to 375°F. Lightly grease a baking sheet.

On the baking sheet, toss the sweet potatoes with the oil, salt, paprika, and rosemary. Spread out in an even layer. Bake for 20 to 30 minutes, or until the potatoes are cooked through and lightly browned.

NUTRITION PER SERVING

133 calories / 24 g carbohydrates / 4 g fiber / 7 g sugars / 2 g protein / 4 g total fat / 0.5 g saturated fat / 652 mg sodium

CHOCOLATE BOCK CARROTS

Carrots are rich in potassium, folate, vitamin K, and beta-carotene. And who doesn't love an excuse to cook with beer? (Which, by the way, has significant amounts of magnesium, selenium, potassium, and phosphorous.)

MAKES 6 SERVINGS // TOTAL TIME: 45 MINUTES

- 4   tablespoons unsalted butter
- 2   pounds rainbow carrots, peeled and cut into 2" × ½" sticks
- 8   fresh sage leaves
- 1   sprig fresh rosemary
- 2   sprigs fresh thyme
- 1   bay leaf
   Salt and ground black pepper, to taste
- ½   cup Samuel Adams Chocolate Bock (or other dark beer)
   Flaky sea salt, to taste

In a large skillet over medium heat, melt the butter. Cook the butter for 5 minutes, or until it turns golden and smells nutty. Stir in the carrots, sage, rosemary, thyme, and bay leaf. Cook, stirring occasionally, for 25 minutes, or until the carrots are tender. Season with salt and pepper. Pour in the beer and cook for 5 minutes, or until the carrots are glazed.

With a slotted spoon, transfer the carrots to a platter. Drizzle with the sauce from the skillet and top with flaky sea salt.

NUTRITION PER SERVING	137 calories / 15 g carbohydrates / 4 g fiber / 7 g sugars / 2 g protein / 8 g total fat / 5 g saturated fat / 186 mg sodium

ROASTED CHICKPEAS WITH CABBAGE SLAW

Spice up your lunch with a fiber-packed dish that will keep you away from the vending machine. The dressing packs a flavorful punch, so use it sparingly. "I make a double batch, top with sesame seeds, and enjoy for lunch throughout the week," says recipe developer and runner Amy Cantor.

MAKES 4 SERVINGS // TOTAL TIME: 1 HOUR

FOR THE CHICKPEAS

1   can (15 ounces) chickpeas, rinsed and drained
3   cloves garlic, unpeeled
    Drizzle of olive oil
    Kosher salt, to taste

FOR THE SLAW

2   cups shredded cabbage
2   cups shredded Brussels sprouts
1   tablespoon toasted sesame oil
    Kosher salt, to taste
    Sesame seeds (optional)

FOR THE DRESSING

    Juice of 1 lemon
1   tablespoon white miso
1   tablespoon finely chopped fresh ginger
1   teaspoon honey
⅓   cup extra-virgin olive oil
    Kosher salt, to taste

TO MAKE THE CHICKPEAS: Preheat the oven to 400°F. Transfer the chickpeas to paper towels and rub gently, removing some of the skins and drying the chickpeas. Spread the chickpeas on a foil-lined baking sheet along with the cloves of garlic. Drizzle with the olive oil and toss. Spread the chickpeas out in an even layer with the garlic throughout. Roast for 35 to 40 minutes, or until the chickpeas are crisp to the touch. Sprinkle with salt to taste. Reserve the roasted garlic for the dressing.

TO MAKE THE SLAW: In a large bowl, toss the cabbage and Brussels sprouts with the sesame oil and salt to taste, and massage for 2 minutes, or until the vegetables begin to soften.

TO MAKE THE DRESSING: Peel the reserved roasted garlic and transfer to a food processor with the lemon juice, miso, ginger, and honey. Pulse until combined. With the motor running, slowly drizzle in the olive oil until emulsified. Season to taste with salt.

Top the slaw with the roasted chickpeas and toss with enough dressing to lightly coat. Sprinkle with sesame seeds, if desired.

NUTRITION PER SERVING

370 calories / 29 g carbohydrates / 8 g fiber / 7 g sugars / 9 g protein / 26 g total fat / 3.5 g saturated fat / 903 mg sodium

ROASTED TOMATOES STUFFED WITH QUINOA AND HERBS

Quinoa is the only grain that is a complete protein, which means it provides all nine essential amino acids needed to build protein. Add tomatoes and you've got a protein- and antioxidant-packed side dish. Serve hot or at room temperature.

MAKES 4 SERVINGS // TOTAL TIME: 30 MINUTES

¼ **cup quinoa, rinsed**

⅔ **cup low-sodium vegetable broth**

4 **tomatoes (about 1⅔ pounds)**

⅛ **teaspoon ground black pepper**

2 **tablespoons crumbled feta cheese**

2 **tablespoons finely chopped fresh basil**

2 **tablespoons finely chopped fresh parsley**

1 **tablespoon finely chopped fresh mint**

1 **teaspoon extra-virgin olive oil**

1 **teaspoon fresh lemon juice**

¼ **teaspoon kosher salt**

Preheat the oven to 400°F.

In a small saucepan, combine the quinoa and broth. Bring to a boil over medium-high heat and stir well. Reduce to a simmer, cover, and cook for 10 to 15 minutes, or until the quinoa is tender and the broth has been absorbed.

Meanwhile, slice the top quarter off the tomatoes and set aside. Use a spoon to scoop out the seeds and pulp from the tomatoes, leaving a sturdy shell. Discard the seeds and pulp. Place the tomatoes in an 8" × 8" baking dish. Season with the pepper.

In a medium bowl, combine the cheese, basil, parsley, mint, oil, lemon juice, and salt. Cut around the stem on the reserved tomato tops and discard the stems. Finely chop the tomato tops and add them to the filling. When the quinoa has finished cooking, stir it into the filling. Stuff each tomato shell with a generous ⅓ cup of the filling. Bake the tomatoes for 12 minutes, or until warmed through.

NUTRITION PER SERVING

101 calories / 15 g carbohydrates / 3 g fiber / 6 g sugars / 4 g protein / 3 g total fat / 1 g saturated fat / 207 mg sodium

COLLARD SPRING ROLLS WITH PEANUT DIPPING SAUCE

This Asian-inspired vegan side (or appetizer) is a great source of high-quality plant protein, thanks to tofu and peanut butter. Beets are high in potassium and fiber but low in calories. And using collard greens instead of rice paper is a sneaky way to up your B-vitamin intake.

MAKES 4 SERVINGS // TOTAL TIME: 1 HOUR 30 MINUTES

FOR THE SPRING ROLLS

- ⅔ **cup brown rice**
- 1 **block (12 to 14 ounces) extra-firm tofu, drained**
- 2 **tablespoons reduced-sodium tamari**
- 12 **large collard leaves**
- 1½ **cups shredded red cabbage**
- 1 **medium golden beet, peeled and grated**
- ¾ **cup coarsely chopped fresh cilantro**

FOR THE DIPPING SAUCE

- ¼ **cup natural peanut butter**
- 3 **tablespoons reduced-sodium tamari**
- 3 **tablespoons water**
- 3 **tablespoons apple cider vinegar**
- 1 **tablespoon toasted sesame oil**

TO MAKE THE SPRING ROLLS: Cook the brown rice according to the package directions. Preheat the oven to 400°F. Line a baking sheet with foil and grease lightly with olive oil.

Meanwhile, gently press the tofu between 2 kitchen towels to remove any excess water, about 15 minutes. Cut the tofu into 12 planks that are ⅓" thick. Spread the tofu planks on the baking sheet so they don't touch. Roast for 15 minutes, or until lightly golden. Drizzle the tamari over the tofu, flip, and return to the oven to roast for 15 minutes, or until the top is lightly golden.

Remove the hard stem from each collard leaf. Carefully shave off some of the rib that runs down the center of the leaf so that it is closer to the same thickness as the leaf.

TO MAKE THE DIPPING SAUCE: In a small bowl, whisk together the peanut butter, tamari, water, vinegar, and oil. Add more water to thin the dressing, if needed.

TO ASSEMBLE: Lay the collard leaves flat. Leaving 1" empty from the bottom, divide the rice, tofu, cabbage, beet, and cilantro among the leaves. Fold up the bottom 1" of the leaf, fold the sides into the center, and roll up the leaf like a burrito. Serve with peanut dipping sauce.

NUTRITION PER SERVING (3 ROLLS)

417 calories / 40 g carbohydrates / 8 g fiber / 5 g sugars / 22 g protein / 19 g total fat / 2.5 g saturated fat / 983 mg sodium

SQUASH MASHED POTATOES

You don't need a heaping bowl of pasta to carb load before a long run or race. Potatoes are an excellent source of nutrition—when they're not fried and covered in salt. Add butternut squash to your mash and you'll have a healthy side dish that packs in the fiber, protein, and vitamin A.

MAKES 4 SERVINGS // TOTAL TIME: 20 MINUTES

1   pound butternut squash, peeled and cubed
1   pound russet potatoes, peeled and cubed
¼   cup grated Parmesan cheese
1   tablespoon unsalted butter
½   teaspoon salt
⅛   teaspoon ground nutmeg
    Ground black pepper, to taste

Bring 1" of water to a boil over high heat. Insert a steamer basket and steam the squash and potatoes for 15 minutes, or until tender. Drain. Return them to the pot and mash with the cheese, butter, salt, and nutmeg. Season with pepper.

NUTRITION PER SERVING 180 calories / 32 g carbohydrates / 4 g fiber / 4 g sugars / 5 g protein / 5 g total fat / 3 g saturated fat / 376 mg sodium

THE RUNNER'S WORLD VEGETARIAN COOKBOOK

ROASTED CURRY CAULIFLOWER

Cauliflower is in the limelight right now, and with good reason. Like other cruciferous veggies (think broccoli and Brussels sprouts), cauliflower has compounds that may inhibit cancer cell growth. Add curry for unique flavor and an anti-inflammatory effect.

MAKES 4 SERVINGS // TOTAL TIME: 20 MINUTES

- 1   medium head cauliflower, broken into florets
- 1   tablespoon olive oil
- 1   teaspoon curry powder
- ½   teaspoon salt
- ¼   teaspoon ground black pepper

Preheat the oven to 450°F. Spread the florets on a baking sheet. Drizzle with the oil. Sprinkle with the curry powder, salt, and pepper. Toss well to coat. Roast for 15 to 20 minutes, or until the cauliflower is tender and browned.

SIDE DISHES

NUTRITION PER SERVING   68 calories / 7 g carbohydrates / 3 g fiber / 3 g sugars / 3 g protein / 4 g total fat / 0.5 g saturated fat / 332 mg sodium

DOUBLE-BAKED
SWEET POTATO SKINS

Potato skins can be a healthy dish when you use vitamin-A packed sweet potatoes. Feta cheese, like other full-fat dairy, is high in calories and fat, but because it has such a powerful flavor, you can use less without sacrificing taste. Double or triple this recipe if you're hosting a prerace dinner.

MAKES 6 SERVINGS // TOTAL TIME: 1 HOUR 30 MINUTES

3	sweet potatoes (8 ounces each), well scrubbed
1	tablespoon olive oil
½	cup crumbled feta cheese
½	teaspoon ground chipotle or other chili powder
6	lime wedges, for serving

Preheat the oven to 425°F. Line a baking sheet with foil.

Place the sweet potatoes on the baking sheet and bake for 1 hour, or until fork-tender but not mushy. Reduce the heat to 400°F.

When the sweet potatoes are cool enough to handle, halve lengthwise and scoop out most of the flesh, leaving a ¼" shell. Then halve them lengthwise again. Drizzle the oil over the flesh side of the potatoes. Bake, flesh side down, for 20 minutes. Turn flesh side up and sprinkle with the cheese and ground chipotle. Bake for 5 minutes, or until the skins are crisp and the cheese has melted. Serve with lime wedges.

NUTRITION PER SERVING 83 calories / 8 g carbohydrates / 1 g fiber / 3 g sugars / 2 g protein / 5 g total fat / 2 g saturated fat / 160 mg sodium

SOBA PANCAKE WITH SCALLIONS AND GINGER

This flavorful soba noodle pancake is great as a side to a veggie stir-fry or as an appetizer.

MAKES 6 SERVINGS // TOTAL TIME: 40 MINUTES

8   ounces soba noodles

¼   cup minced scallions, plus more for garnish

2   tablespoons soy sauce

1   teaspoon dark sesame oil

1   teaspoon grated fresh ginger

4   drops chili oil

2   tablespoons peanut oil

Hot pepper sauce (optional)

Preheat the oven to 500°F.

Bring a medium pot of salted water to a boil. Cook the noodles according to the package directions. Drain and place in a bowl. Add the scallions, soy sauce, sesame oil, ginger, and chili oil. Stir to coat the noodles.

In a 10" cast-iron (or other ovenproof) skillet over medium heat, heat the peanut oil. Add the noodle mixture, pressing down and spreading it evenly across the bottom of the skillet. Place the skillet on the lowest oven rack. Bake for 20 to 25 minutes, or until the pancake is crisp and dark golden. Slide the pancake out and cut into 6 wedges. Top with more scallions. Serve hot, with hot pepper sauce, if desired.

NUTRITION PER SERVING   178 calories / 29 g carbohydrates / 0 g fiber / 0 g sugars / 6 g protein / 6 g total fat / 1 g saturated fat / 478 mg sodium

RATATOUILLE

Ratatouille, like stir-fry, is an easy way to up your veggie intake, and eggplant is a good source of potassium for muscle function. This dish, which can be served warm or cold, is great as a side, or double the portions and serve it as a main over quinoa.

MAKES 4 SERVINGS // TOTAL TIME: 50 MINUTES

2	tablespoons olive oil
1	large onion, halved and thinly sliced
2	cloves garlic, minced
1	small eggplant, cubed
2	medium green bell peppers, coarsely chopped
4	large tomatoes, coarsely chopped
3	zucchini, cut into ½" slices
2	tablespoons chopped fresh parsley
1	teaspoon chopped fresh basil
½	teaspoon dried oregano
½	teaspoon fresh thyme
½	teaspoon salt

In a large saucepan over medium heat, heat the oil. Add the onion and garlic and cook for 7 minutes, or until soft. Add the eggplant and stir until coated with the oil. Add the peppers and stir to combine. Cover the pan and cook for 10 minutes, stirring occasionally to avoid sticking. Add the tomatoes, zucchini, parsley, basil, oregano, thyme, and salt and mix well. Cover, reduce the heat to low, and cook for 15 to 20 minutes, or until the eggplant is tender but not mushy. Taste and adjust the seasoning, if needed.

NUTRITION PER SERVING

176 calories / 25 g carbohydrates / 8 g fiber / 15 g sugars / 6 g protein / 8 g total fat / 1 g saturated fat / 319 mg sodium

5-MINUTE COLESLAW

Raisins add extra fiber and a hint of natural sweetness to this slaw, while almonds are a great source of heart-healthy fats. Serve as a side dish, atop a veggie burger, or in grilled cheese for added crunch.

MAKES 4 SERVINGS // TOTAL TIME: 5 MINUTES

- 2 **cups preshredded cabbage or coleslaw mixture**
- 2 **cups broccoli slaw mixture, chopped slightly**
- ¼ **cup golden raisins**
- ¼ **cup slivered almonds**
- ⅔ **cup prepared poppy seed salad dressing**

In a large serving bowl, combine the cabbage, broccoli slaw, raisins, almonds, and salad dressing. Toss to coat evenly.

PRO TIP

Depending on the type of dressing you choose, this dish could also be vegan, gluten-free, and/or allergen-free.

NUTRITION PER SERVING

275 calories / 24 g carbohydrates / 3 g fiber / 18 g sugars / 4 g protein / 19 g total fat / 3 g saturated fat / 368 mg sodium

HERBED COLESLAW

Fresh herbs add a unique flavor to ordinary coleslaw. To make this dish vegan, use vegan mayo instead. Serve atop a veggie burger for flavor and crunch.

MAKES 4 SERVINGS // TOTAL TIME: 10 MINUTES, PLUS 1 HOUR CHILLING TIME

2   cups shredded cabbage
1   cup chopped celery
1   carrot, shredded
2   sprigs fresh dill, chopped
2   tablespoons finely sliced fresh basil
¼   teaspoon salt
3   tablespoons mayonnaise
2   tablespoons white wine vinegar
1   teaspoon poppy seeds (optional)
¼   teaspoon ground black pepper

In a large bowl, combine the cabbage, celery, carrot, dill, and basil. Sprinkle with the salt and toss well. In a small bowl, combine the mayonnaise, vinegar, poppy seeds (if using), and pepper. Add to the vegetables and toss again. Chill for at least 1 hour before serving to allow the flavors to blend.

NUTRITION PER SERVING   57 calories / 5 g carbohydrates / 2 g fiber / 3 g sugars / 1 g protein / 4 g total fat / 0.5 g saturated fat / 254 mg sodium

VEGAN "CREAMED" SPINACH

Spinach is a runner superfood thanks to its high levels of vitamins A and C, iron, and magnesium. Protein-rich tofu and soy milk make this dish creamy without any dairy—that's why this is a vegan favorite.

MAKES 4 SERVINGS // TOTAL TIME: 20 MINUTES

1   **cup soft silken tofu**
2   **packages (10 ounces each) frozen whole-leaf spinach**
½   **cup water**
1   **teaspoon salt**
½   **teaspoon ground black pepper**
⅛   **teaspoon ground nutmeg**
1   **cup plain soy milk, warmed**

Line a colander with several thicknesses of paper towels. Add the tofu and set aside for 10 minutes to drain off excess liquid.

Meanwhile, in a medium saucepan, combine the spinach and water. Bring to a boil over high heat. Reduce the heat to medium-low, cover, and cook for 7 to 10 minutes, or until just tender. Drain the spinach in a colander. Using the back of a large spoon, press against the spinach to remove as much water as possible. (You should be able to remove at least ½ cup.)

Place the drained spinach in a food processor and process until almost smooth. Add the drained tofu, salt, pepper, and nutmeg and process until smooth. Add the soy milk and process until just combined. Serve hot (reheat if necessary).

NUTRITION PER SERVING 105 calories / 11 g carbohydrates / 5 g fiber / 3 g sugars / 10 g protein / 4 g total fat / 0.5 g saturated fat / 730 mg sodium

CUBAN RICE AND BEANS

Beans and rice go hand in hand for flavor and nutrition: Together they make a complete plant-based protein. Use brown rice for extra nutrients like B vitamins, iron, and magnesium. This dish is a great source of complex carbohydrates, but it's also high in fiber, so don't eat it immediately before a run or race.

MAKES 4 SERVINGS // TOTAL TIME: 50 MINUTES

½ cup brown rice

4 teaspoons extra-virgin olive oil

1 medium onion, thinly sliced

1 large red bell pepper, sliced

3 cloves garlic, minced

1 teaspoon dried basil

1 teaspoon ground cumin

½ teaspoon ground coriander

16 grape tomatoes

5 teaspoons white wine vinegar

1 can (15 ounces) black beans, rinsed and drained

1 can (15 ounces) pinto beans, rinsed and drained

¾ teaspoon salt

¼ teaspoon ground black pepper

Cook the rice according to the package directions.

Meanwhile, in a large saucepan over medium-high heat, heat the oil. Add the onion, bell pepper, garlic, basil, cumin, and coriander. Cook, stirring occasionally, for 5 minutes, or until the vegetables begin to soften. Add the tomatoes and cook for 3 minutes, or until they begin to collapse. Add the vinegar and cook for 30 seconds to evaporate. Mix in the black and pinto beans and bring to a boil. Reduce the heat to a simmer, cover, and cook, stirring occasionally, for 30 minutes, or until the vegetables are very tender and the mixture is fairly thick. Season with the salt and black pepper. Serve the bean mixture over the rice.

SIDE DISHES

NUTRITION PER SERVING 280 calories / 47 g carbohydrates / 9 g fiber / 8 g sugars / 10 g protein / 6 g total fat / 1 g saturated fat / 704 mg sodium

ISRAELI COUSCOUS WITH LIME AND MINT

Israeli couscous is larger than regular couscous and has a chewier texture. It's best to choose whole wheat couscous for a boost of fiber, B vitamins, iron, and magnesium.

MAKES 4 SERVINGS // TOTAL TIME: 20 MINUTES

1 tablespoon olive oil

3 cloves garlic, thinly sliced

1 teaspoon finely chopped fresh jalapeño chile pepper

1¼ cups whole wheat Israeli couscous

2½ cups boiling water

1½ teaspoons grated lime zest

¾ teaspoon salt

¼ cup chopped fresh mint

¼ cup chopped fresh chives

In a medium saucepan over medium heat, heat the oil. Add the garlic and jalapeño pepper and cook for 1 minute, or until the garlic is tender. Add the couscous and stir to coat. Add the boiling water, lime zest, and salt. Bring to a boil, reduce the heat to a simmer, cover, and cook for 12 minutes, or until the couscous is tender and the liquid has been absorbed. Using a fork, stir in the mint and chives, and fluff the couscous.

NUTRITION PER SERVING 248 calories / 48 g carbohydrates / 8 g fiber / 1 g sugars / 9 g protein / 4 g total fat / 0.5 g saturated fat / 442 mg sodium

SESAME BOK CHOY

Unsure how to cook this staple from our farm share, we knew we couldn't go wrong with sesame oil for Asian flavor. Bok choy is a good source of many nutrients, including vitamins A, C, and K, as well as glucosinolates, which may be associated with decreased cancer risk. This dish is great as a side or tossed into a stir-fry.

MAKES 4 SERVINGS // TOTAL TIME: 10 MINUTES

2 tablespoons coconut oil

3 cloves garlic, minced

1 teaspoon grated fresh ginger, or ½ teaspoon ground ginger

¼ to ½ teaspoon red pepper flakes

1½ pounds bok choy (about 2 medium bunches), cleaned, trimmed, and cut on the diagonal into 1" pieces

1 tablespoon soy sauce

2 teaspoons water

1 teaspoon rice vinegar

½ teaspoon toasted sesame oil

½ teaspoon sesame seeds

In a large skillet over medium-high heat, melt the coconut oil. Add the garlic, ginger, and red pepper flakes and cook, stirring constantly, for 30 seconds, or until fragrant but not brown.

Stir in the bok choy and coat in the garlic-ginger mixture. Add the soy sauce, water, and vinegar. Cover and cook for 1 minute, or until steam builds. Uncover and cook, stirring occasionally, for 2 minutes, or until the greens are wilted and the stalks are tender-crisp. If there is still liquid in the skillet, continue cooking until it's evaporated.

Remove from the heat, stir in the sesame oil, and sprinkle with the sesame seeds.

NUTRITION PER SERVING   94 calories / 5 g carbohydrates / 2 g fiber / 2 g sugars / 3 g protein / 8 g total fat / 6 g saturated fat / 331 mg sodium

VEGGIE ROLLS WITH MANGO-GINGER DIPPING SAUCE

Up the ante of a traditional veggie roll with radish sprouts, carrots, snow peas, and lettuce. If you can't find mango fruit spread, try apricot, peach, pineapple, or plum. For easy rolling, avoid rice paper labeled "thin" or "mung."

MAKES 8 SERVINGS // TOTAL TIME: 25 MINUTES

FOR THE DIPPING SAUCE

¼   cup mango fruit spread
2   tablespoons low-sodium soy sauce
1   tablespoon seasoned rice vinegar
    Finely grated zest of 1 small lime
1   tablespoon fresh lime juice
½   teaspoon finely grated fresh ginger
¼   teaspoon hot pepper sauce

FOR THE ROLLS

¼   cup fresh cilantro leaves
16 snow peas, ends trimmed
8   small, tender leaves Boston or romaine lettuce
8   large rice paper wrappers
3   ounces baked tofu (sesame ginger or teriyaki flavor preferred), thinly sliced
2   cups radish sprouts
½   cup shredded carrots

TO MAKE THE DIPPING SAUCE: In a small bowl, whisk together the fruit spread, soy sauce, rice vinegar, lime zest, lime juice, ginger, and hot pepper sauce. Set aside.

TO MAKE THE ROLLS: Rinse the cilantro, snow peas, and lettuce and pat dry. Fill a shallow bowl with hot water. Dip 1 rice paper wrapper at a time into the water until it becomes pliable, about 5 seconds. Lay the wet wrapper on a damp towel and let it rest for a few seconds until it's soft and slightly tacky.

Place 2 to 4 cilantro leaves on the lower third of the wrapper, 1" or so from the edge. Cover with 2 or 3 tofu slices. Top with ¼ cup sprouts, 1 tablespoon carrots, and 2 snow peas. Fold 1 lettuce leaf in half and place on top.

Fold the bottom of the wrapper over the filling. Tuck in the sides toward the center and roll upward tightly. Repeat until all of the wrappers and ingredients have been used. Cut each roll in half. Serve immediately with the dipping sauce.

NUTRITION PER SERVING	70 calories / 9 g carbohydrates / 1 g fiber / 6 g sugars / 3 g protein / 3 g total fat / 0 g saturated fat / 218 mg sodium

SPRING RISOTTO

Fresh peas really make the flavor in this dish pop. If you don't have access to fresh ones, opt for frozen peas, which retain their nutrition and are often packaged just after they're picked. You can give the "risotto treatment" to virtually any grain, such as fiber-rich brown rice, using the method here, cooking until the grain is just tender.

MAKES 4 SERVINGS // TOTAL TIME: 40 MINUTES

- 4 **cups low-sodium vegetable broth**
- 1 **tablespoon unsalted butter**
- 1 **tablespoon olive oil**
- 1 **onion, chopped**
- ½ **teaspoon salt**
- 1½ **cups Arborio or carnaroli rice**
- 12 **ounces fresh peas in the pod, shelled, or 1 cup frozen peas**
- 1 **tablespoon fresh lemon juice**
- ¼ **cup grated Parmesan cheese**

In a small saucepan over high heat, bring the broth to a boil. Reduce the heat to low and cover to keep warm.

Meanwhile, in a large saucepan or skillet over medium-low heat, melt the butter and oil. Add the onion and salt. Cook, stirring occasionally, for 4 minutes, or until the onion is translucent. Add the rice and stir for 1 minute to coat the rice in the butter-oil mixture.

Add about 1½ cups of the broth and adjust the heat to maintain a good simmer. Stir frequently, until most of the liquid has been absorbed. Add ½ cup of the remaining broth and continue simmering and stirring until absorbed. Continue in this manner, adding the peas with the final ½ cup broth. Simmer and stir for 4 minutes, or until the rice is just tender. Stir in the lemon juice and cheese. Serve immediately.

NUTRITION PER SERVING

435 calories / 73 g carbohydrates / 3 g fiber / 4 g sugars / 16 g protein / 10 g total fat / 4 g saturated fat / 988 mg sodium

QUINOA AND RED LENTIL KITCHARI

Kitchari makes a great side dish or main course (double the portions!) when you want warm, healthy comfort food. "I like to swap carrots for sweet potatoes, or even use both, for an extra boost of vitamin A and fiber," says Chris Mosier, a pro duathlete and the first known transgender athlete to represent a US men's team in international competition. Make sure to salt to taste individual portions to avoid oversalting the entire dish. Use olive oil instead of ghee to make this dish vegan.

MAKES 6 SERVINGS // TOTAL TIME: 40 MINUTES, PLUS 1 HOUR SOAKING TIME

½   cup quinoa, rinsed

¾   cup red lentils, rinsed

1   tablespoon olive oil or ghee

½   white onion, finely chopped

3   carrots, sliced ¼" thick

1   teaspoon curry powder

1   teaspoon ground coriander

1   teaspoon ground cumin

3   to 4 cups water

½   bunch kale, chopped, or 2 cups chopped kale

Sea salt, to taste

In separate bowls of water, soak the quinoa and lentils for 1 hour. Drain the quinoa and drain and rinse the lentils.

In a large, heavy-bottomed saucepan over medium heat, heat the oil or ghee. Add the onion and carrots and cook for 3 minutes, or until softened. Stir in the curry powder, coriander, and cumin.

Add the quinoa, lentils, and 3 cups of the water. Bring to a boil, cover, reduce the heat, and simmer for 10 minutes.

Stir in the kale, adding up to 1 cup more water if needed to keep the mixture loose. Simmer, uncovered, for 15 minutes, or until thick and all the water has been absorbed. Season with salt.

NUTRITION PER SERVING   187 calories / 29 g carbohydrates / 6 g fiber / 3 g sugars / 10 g protein / 4 g total fat / 0.5 g saturated fat / 103 mg sodium

5 MAIN DISHES

CURRY EGG SALAD SANDWICH

When you make your own egg salad, you control the ingredients, and that means you don't need to slather on the high-fat mayo. Swapping out the mayo for Greek yogurt gives you the same texture plus extra calcium with a fraction of the fat. The curry powder and raisins add flavor and a touch of natural sweetness to this protein- and vitamin D–packed sandwich.

MAKES 2 SERVINGS // TOTAL TIME: 10 MINUTES

¼ **cup low-fat plain Greek yogurt**

2 **tablespoons golden raisins**

1 **teaspoon Dijon mustard**

2 **scallions, sliced**

½ **teaspoon curry powder**

⅛ **teaspoon salt**

⅛ **teaspoon ground black pepper**

4 **eggs, hard-cooked and chopped**

2 **whole grain bagels, cut in half**

4 **slices avocado**

¼ **cup fresh cilantro, coarsely chopped**

In a bowl, stir together the yogurt, raisins, mustard, scallions, curry powder, salt, and pepper. Gently stir in the eggs.

Divide the egg mixture between 2 bagel halves. Top each with an equal amount of avocado and cilantro. Top with the remaining bagel halves.

NUTRITION PER SERVING

421 calories / 51 g carbohydrates / 9 g fiber / 12 g sugars / 22 g protein / 17 g total fat / 4.5 g saturated fat / 545 mg sodium

GRILLED VEGETABLE POLENTA CASSEROLE

When summer is in full swing, you have dozens of nutrient-packed fresh veggies to choose from. Olympic medalist Deena Kastor throws her favorites into this casserole, but you don't need to feel restricted by the veggies listed here. You can use whatever you like or have on hand. Kastor makes this dish for weekend get-togethers and serves it with a fresh salad and crusty bread. To save time, you can use two 16-ounce tubes of premade polenta cut into ¼" slices, instead of making your own.

MAKES 10 SERVINGS // TOTAL TIME: 1 HOUR 30 MINUTES

- 1 **large eggplant, cut lengthwise into ½"-thick slices**
- 2 **yellow squash, cut lengthwise into ¼"-thick slices**
- 4 **portobello mushrooms, stems discarded**
- 1 **bunch asparagus, trimmed**
- 2 **tablespoons extra-virgin olive oil**
- 8 **cups water**
- 1 **teaspoon salt**
- 2 **cups polenta or coarse cornmeal**
- 1½ **cups marinara sauce, divided**
- ½ **cup crumbled goat cheese (2 ounces)**
- ¼ **cup coarsely chopped fresh basil**

Heat a grill to medium-high heat. Brush the eggplant, squash, mushrooms, and asparagus with the oil. Grill the vegetables for 8 to 10 minutes, or until tender, turning the squash, mushrooms, and asparagus after 4 minutes and the eggplant after 5 or 6 minutes. Remove the vegetables from the grill. Slice each mushroom into 8 strips.

In a large pot over high heat, combine the water and salt and bring to a boil. Whisk in the polenta or cornmeal in a slow, steady stream. Reduce the heat to low and cook, stirring, for 20 to 30 minutes, or until the polenta reaches a thick but spreadable consistency.

Preheat the oven to 375°F. To assemble the casserole, spread ½ cup of the marinara sauce on the bottom of a 13" × 9" baking dish. Add half of the polenta. Layer each of the vegetables atop one another. Spread the remaining polenta over the vegetables. Smother with the remaining 1 cup marinara sauce. Sprinkle with the cheese and basil.

Cover with foil and bake for 30 minutes, or until the sauce starts to bubble. Remove the foil and bake for 10 minutes longer, or until the cheese browns. Let the casserole cool for 5 minutes before cutting.

NUTRITION PER SERVING

254 calories / 36 g carbohydrates / 6 g fiber / 6 g sugars / 10 g protein / 9 g total fat / 3 g saturated fat / 692 mg sodium

DOUBLE PORTOBELLO BURGERS

At your next summer barbecue, broil these giant mushroom caps and add all the summer fixins for a juicy, tasty meal. Portobello mushrooms are also perfect for the grill.

MAKES 4 SERVINGS // TOTAL TIME: 45 MINUTES

8 portobello mushrooms (3 ounces each), stems discarded

⅓ cup extra-virgin olive oil

3 tablespoons balsamic vinegar

2 cloves garlic, finely minced

2 teaspoons fresh thyme leaves, chopped

½ teaspoon coarse salt

4 soft multigrain buns

4 ounces soft goat cheese, crumbled

1 teaspoon truffle oil (optional)

4 slices sweet onion, such as Vidalia or Maui

8 arugula leaves

With a small spoon, scrape the black gills out of the mushroom caps. In a small bowl, stir together the oil, vinegar, garlic, thyme, and salt. Brush on both sides of the mushroom caps, and let the mixture seep in for 20 minutes.

Preheat the broiler. Lightly oil a baking sheet. Arrange the mushrooms in 1 layer, gill side up, on the baking sheet. Broil 6" from the heat for 6 minutes, or until somewhat soft. Turn and broil for 6 minutes more, or until the mushrooms are hot and tender.

To assemble each burger, place a mushroom, gill side up, on a bottom bun. Top with goat cheese and drizzle with ¼ teaspoon truffle oil (if using). Add a second mushroom, gill side down, an onion slice, 2 arugula leaves, and the top bun.

NUTRITION PER SERVING 462 calories / 44 g carbohydrates / 7 g fiber / 12 g sugars / 15 g protein / 28 g total fat / 7.5 g saturated fat / 703 mg sodium

COCOA BLACK BEAN TACOS

Spice up your Taco Tuesday with this chocolaty taco, packed with antioxidants and fiber. Tacos are an easy, tasty way to add nutrients to your plate, thanks to their ability to be stuffed with anything.

MAKES 4 SERVINGS // TOTAL TIME: 25 MINUTES

2 teaspoons canola or grapeseed oil

1 small yellow onion, diced

2 plum (Roma) tomatoes, seeded and diced

1 ripe plantain, peeled and diced

1 can (15 ounces) black beans, rinsed and drained

2 tablespoons unsweetened cocoa powder

½ teaspoon chili powder

½ teaspoon ground cumin

¼ cup water

½ teaspoon kosher salt

½ teaspoon ground black pepper

⅓ cup chopped fresh cilantro

4 tablespoons fresh lime juice, divided

½ cup sour cream

½ avocado

8 small corn tortillas (6" diameter)

1 jarred roasted red bell pepper, thinly sliced

¼ cup hulled pumpkin seeds, toasted

In a skillet over medium heat, heat the oil. Add the onion and cook for 3 minutes, or until soft. Add the tomatoes, plantain, beans, cocoa powder, chili powder, cumin, water, salt, and black pepper and cook for 3 minutes. Stir in the cilantro and 2 tablespoons of the lime juice. Remove from the heat.

In a blender, combine the sour cream, avocado, remaining 2 tablespoons lime juice, and a pinch of salt. Puree until smooth.

Divide the filling among the tortillas and top with the roasted pepper, avocado cream, and pumpkin seeds.

NUTRITION PER SERVING
409 calories / 60 g carbohydrates / 12 g fiber / 12 g sugars / 11 g protein / 16 g total fat / 5 g saturated fat / 488 mg sodium

SMOKY SQUASH FLATBREAD WITH BALSAMIC GLAZE

The sauce for this flatbread is made from frozen winter squash puree, which makes it easy and quick to load up on nutrition. Hazelnuts are a good source of heart-healthy fats and add a little crunch to this meal.

MAKES 4 SERVINGS // TOTAL TIME: 25 MINUTES

FOR THE SAUCE

- 1 package (12 ounces) frozen winter squash puree, thawed
- ½ cup grated Parmesan or pecorino cheese
- 2 cloves garlic, minced
- ¾ teaspoon smoked paprika
- ½ teaspoon ground cumin
- ¼ teaspoon ground nutmeg
- ¼ teaspoon salt
- ¼ teaspoon ground black pepper

FOR THE FLATBREADS AND GLAZE

- ¼ pound Brussels sprouts, stems trimmed
- 1 tablespoon extra-virgin olive oil
- 4 whole wheat naan flatbreads
- ¼ cup crumbled goat cheese (1 ounce)
- ¼ cup chopped hazelnuts (1 ounce)
- ⅓ cup balsamic vinegar
- 2 teaspoons firmly packed light brown sugar

Preheat the oven to 400°F. Line 2 baking sheets with parchment paper or foil.

TO MAKE THE SAUCE: In a small bowl, combine the squash, Parmesan or pecorino cheese, garlic, paprika, cumin, nutmeg, salt, and pepper. Stir until well combined. Set aside.

TO MAKE THE FLATBREADS: In a food processor fitted with a shredding disk, shred the Brussels sprouts. (Alternatively, halve them and then thinly slice with a sharp knife.) In a bowl, toss the shredded sprouts with the oil.

Set the flatbreads on the baking sheets. Spread an even amount of the squash sauce over them, leaving a ½" border uncovered. Top evenly with the Brussels sprouts, goat cheese, and hazelnuts. Bake for 10 minutes, or until the crust is golden brown and the cheese begins to melt.

TO MAKE THE GLAZE: Meanwhile, in a small saucepan, combine the vinegar and brown sugar and bring to a simmer over medium heat. Cook for 6 minutes, or until syrupy and reduced to 2 tablespoons. Serve the flatbreads drizzled with the balsamic glaze.

NUTRITION PER SERVING

431 calories / 56 g carbohydrates / 7 g fiber / 11 g sugars / 16 g protein / 17 g total fat / 5 g saturated fat / 680 mg sodium

TOFU PEANUT STIR-FRY

This vegan spin on a traditional peanut stir-fry will power your runs and your recovery thanks to the plant protein found in tofu and peanuts. Hoisin sauce and seasoned rice vinegar can be found in the Asian aisle in most grocery stores. Keep these on hand for a quick stir-fry on a busy night.

MAKES 4 SERVINGS // TOTAL TIME: 30 MINUTES

1½ cups **instant brown rice**

4 teaspoons **canola oil, divided**

1 package (14 ounces) **extra-firm tofu, drained, pressed, and cut into ½" pieces**

1 **onion, chopped**

1 package (8 ounces) **sliced mushrooms**

3 cloves **garlic, minced**

1 tablespoon **grated fresh ginger**

½ cup **frozen peas**

½ cup **salted dry-roasted peanuts**

⅓ cup **hoisin sauce**

1 tablespoon **seasoned rice vinegar**

3 **scallions, chopped**

Cook the rice according to the package directions.

Meanwhile, in a large skillet over medium-high heat, heat 2 teaspoons of the oil. Add the tofu and cook, turning occasionally, for 8 to 10 minutes, or until lightly browned. Transfer to a plate and set aside.

Return the skillet to the stove and heat the remaining 2 teaspoons oil. Stir in the onion and cook for 1 minute. Add the mushrooms and cook, stirring occasionally, for 5 to 6 minutes, or until lightly browned. Stir in the garlic and ginger and cook for 30 seconds, or until fragrant. Add the peas and peanuts and cook for 1 minute, or until the peas are bright green. Return the tofu to the pan and add the hoisin sauce and vinegar. Cook, stirring, for 1 minute, or until hot.

Remove from the heat and stir in the scallions. Serve over the rice.

PRO TIP

Before adding the tofu to the stir-fry, press it to remove excess moisture (doing so will help the tofu hold its shape). Cut the tofu into slices, then lay the slices on a baking sheet or cutting board lined with paper towels. Cover with more paper towels and press with your hands.

NUTRITION PER SERVING

595 calories / 79 g carbohydrates / 9 g fiber / 11 g sugars / 24 g protein / 22 g total fat / 2.5 g saturated fat / 544 mg sodium

BUTTERNUT SQUASH QUINOA BOWL

Inspired by the Rodale cafeteria, this veggie quinoa bowl is an easy and tasty way to fill up. Quinoa is the only grain that provides a complete protein, which means it has all nine essential amino acids needed to build protein for muscle maintenance. If you prefer a more greens-based bowl, halve the quinoa and double the kale amounts. I like to make a big batch on Sunday and have it for lunch throughout the week. (It can't hurt to top it with sliced avocado, either!)

MAKES 4 SERVINGS // TOTAL TIME: 40 MINUTES

2　cups cubed peeled butternut squash

3　tablespoons olive oil, divided

　　Salt and ground black pepper, to taste

1　cup quinoa, rinsed

1　medium red onion, chopped

1½ cups coarsely chopped kale

1　apple, cored and chopped

½　cup dried cranberries

Preheat the oven to 400°F. On a large baking sheet, toss the butternut squash with 2 tablespoons of the oil and a generous sprinkle of salt and pepper. Roast, stirring halfway, for 25 minutes, or until the squash is browned and tender.

Meanwhile, cook the quinoa according to the package directions.

In a medium skillet over medium heat, heat the remaining 1 tablespoon oil until shimmering. Add the onion and cook for 5 minutes, or until softened. Stir in the kale, cover, and cook for 3 minutes, or just until the kale wilts slightly.

In a serving bowl, toss together the kale mixture, squash, and quinoa. Season with salt and pepper, and top with the apple and cranberries.

NUTRITION PER SERVING

371 calories / 59 g carbohydrates / 7 g fiber / 19 g sugars / 8 g protein / 13 g total fat / 2 g saturated fat / 167 mg sodium

VEGETARIAN SOUVLAKI WITH PITA WRAPS

Load your pitas with veggies for a refreshing summer lunch or dinner. Eggplants, green peppers, and pineapples are high in antioxidants, and mushrooms are a good source of selenium for bone health.

MAKES 4 SERVINGS // TOTAL TIME: 40 MINUTES

½ large eggplant, cubed

12 large button mushrooms

1 green bell pepper, cut into 1" pieces

6 pineapple rings, quartered

2 tablespoons balsamic vinegar

1 tablespoon chopped fresh oregano, or 1 teaspoon dried

2 teaspoons olive oil

1 teaspoon minced garlic

8 large pitas

In a large bowl, combine the eggplant, mushrooms, bell pepper, pineapple, vinegar, oregano, oil, and garlic. Marinate for 20 minutes at room temperature, stirring frequently.

Prepare the grill for medium-high heat. Thread the vegetables and pineapple on 4 metal skewers, alternating colors. Reserve any remaining marinade. Grill, turning once, for 10 minutes, or until lightly browned, basting with the leftover marinade.

Warm the pitas on the grill, turning once. Wrap 1 pita around each shish kebab and remove the skewer.

NUTRITION PER SERVING 461 calories / 93 g carbohydrates / 7 g fiber / 20 g sugars / 15 g protein / 4 g total fat / 1 g saturated fat / 652 mg sodium

VEGGIE "MEAT" LOAF

If you've somehow got leftovers from dinner, this "meat" loaf makes a great next-day sandwich. Serve a slice in a whole wheat pita with lettuce, tomato, and a little mayonnaise. For the best way to remove excess water from tofu, see the Pro Tip on page 147.

MAKES 4 SERVINGS // TOTAL TIME: 1 HOUR 15 MINUTES, PLUS 10 MINUTES RESTING TIME

1 teaspoon olive oil

1 small onion, finely chopped

6 ounces baby spinach leaves

1 carrot, shredded

1½ teaspoons salt-free garlic-herb seasoning blend

1 slice sprouted whole grain bread, torn into pieces

7 ounces firm tofu, drained, pressed, and cut into 1" cubes

1 can (15 ounces) chickpeas, rinsed and drained

1 cup cooked brown rice

1 large egg white

½ cup ketchup, divided

3 teaspoons Dijon mustard, divided

Preheat the oven to 375°F. Line a rimmed baking sheet with foil and coat with cooking spray.

In a large nonstick skillet over medium-high heat, heat the oil. Cook the onion, stirring, for 5 minutes, or until softened. Add the spinach, carrot, and seasoning. Cook, stirring constantly, for 2 minutes, or until the spinach wilts. Transfer to a large bowl and let cool for 10 minutes.

Place the bread in a food processor and pulse to form crumbs. Add to the bowl with the vegetables. Add the tofu and chickpeas to the processor and pulse until mashed. Add to the bowl along with the brown rice, egg white, ¼ cup of the ketchup, and 2 teaspoons of the mustard. Stir until well blended and the mixture holds together. Let stand for 5 minutes.

Shape into a 7" × 3½" loaf on the center of the baking sheet. In a small bowl, combine the remaining ¼ cup ketchup and 1 teaspoon mustard. Spread over the top of the loaf.

Bake for 50 minutes, or until cooked through. Remove from the oven and let rest for 10 minutes before slicing into 8 slices with a serrated knife.

NUTRITION PER SERVING (2 SLICES)

316 calories / 52 g carbohydrates / 10 g fiber / 13 g sugars / 15 g protein / 6 g total fat / 1 g saturated fat / 500 mg sodium

VEGGIE ENGLISH MUFFIN PIZZA

A veggie-loaded pizza should not be deemed junk food. But if you need a snack (versus a prerace dinner), an English muffin pizza is a great lower-calorie way to go. Pile your favorite veggies high. And you'll be surprised how far 2 tablespoons of shredded mozzarella goes when it's melted. For a little extra fiber, swap a white muffin out for a whole wheat one.

MAKES 1 SERVING // TOTAL TIME: 15 MINUTES

1   **English muffin, split**
¼   **cup plain tomato sauce**
¼   **cup chopped mushrooms**
2   **tablespoons chopped green bell pepper**
2   **tablespoons chopped onion**
2   **tablespoons shredded reduced-fat mozzarella cheese**

Preheat the oven or toaster oven to 350°F. Toast the muffin halves. Evenly divide the sauce, mushrooms, pepper, onion, and cheese between the muffin halves. Bake for 3 minutes, or until the cheese is melted.

MAIN DISHES

NUTRITION PER SERVING

199 calories / 33 g carbohydrates / 3 g fiber / 4 g sugars / 10 g protein / 3 g total fat / 1.5 g saturated fat / 688 mg sodium

CURRY-SPICED VEGGIE BURGERS

Spice up your homemade veggie burger with curry, an excellent antioxidant thanks to its turmeric content. Serve on whole wheat buns with a salad or slaw on the side.

MAKES 6 SERVINGS // TOTAL TIME: 30 MINUTES

2 tablespoons olive or canola oil, divided

1 medium onion, chopped (about 1 cup)

1 teaspoon curry powder

½ teaspoon ground coriander

½ teaspoon crushed fennel seeds

1½ cups chopped white button mushrooms

1 can (15 ounces) chickpeas, rinsed and drained

1 medium carrot, grated (about 1 cup)

¼ cup chopped walnuts

3 tablespoons chopped fresh cilantro

½ teaspoon salt

¼ teaspoon ground black pepper

Flour, for dusting

In a medium nonstick skillet over medium-high heat, heat 1 tablespoon of the oil. Add the onion, curry powder, coriander, and fennel. Cook, stirring frequently, for 2 minutes, or until the onion starts to soften. Add the mushrooms. Stir to mix. Cover and cook for 4 minutes, or until the liquid pools in the pan. Uncover and cook for 3 minutes, or until the liquid has evaporated.

Transfer the mixture to the bowl of a food processor. Add the chickpeas. Pulse until well chopped. Transfer to a bowl.

Add the carrot, walnuts, cilantro, salt, and pepper and mix well. Lightly dust your hands with flour. Shape the mixture into six 4"-wide patties.

In a large skillet over medium heat, heat the remaining 1 tablespoon oil. Place the patties in the pan. Cook, turning once when browned on the bottom, for 8 minutes, or until heated through.

NUTRITION PER SERVING

165 calories / 17 g carbohydrates / 5 g fiber / 4 g sugars / 6 g protein / 9 g total fat / 1 g saturated fat / 209 mg sodium

SPAGHETTI SQUASH WITH VEGGIE GRATIN

Squash is an excellent source of complex carbohydrates that's lower in calories and carbs than traditional pasta. Mix with veggies for a "pasta" primavera before your next race. If you're running long, give yourself three servings to get the calories you need.

MAKES 6 SERVINGS // TOTAL TIME: 1 HOUR 35 MINUTES

- 1 **spaghetti squash (about 3 pounds)**
- 1 **teaspoon olive oil**
- 2 **medium zucchini, finely chopped**
- 1 **cup sliced mushrooms**
- ¼ **cup chopped spring onion**
- 2 **cloves garlic, minced**
- 1 **can (14½ ounces) no-salt-added diced tomatoes with Italian seasonings**
- ¾ **cup shredded reduced-fat mozzarella cheese (3 ounces)**
- ¼ **cup chopped fresh parsley**
- ½ **teaspoon salt**
- ½ **teaspoon ground black pepper**

Preheat the oven to 350°F. Slice the squash in half lengthwise and scoop out the seeds. Place the squash, cut sides down, in a 13" × 9" baking dish. Add water to the dish to a depth of ½". Bake for 50 minutes, or until fork-tender. Remove the squash from the oven, discard the water, and increase the heat to 450°F.

When the squash is cool enough to handle, scrape with a fork to remove the spaghetti-like strands. Coat the baking dish with cooking spray. Return the pulp to the baking dish.

Meanwhile, in a large nonstick skillet over medium-high heat, heat the oil. Add the zucchini, mushrooms, onion, and garlic and cook, stirring frequently, for 10 minutes, or until the vegetables are tender. Remove from the heat.

Stir in the tomatoes (with juice), cheese, parsley, salt, and pepper. Add to the baking dish with the squash and toss to combine. Spread evenly in the baking dish. Bake for 15 minutes, or until hot and bubbling.

NUTRITION PER SERVING 125 calories / 19 g carbohydrates / 5 g fiber / 9 g sugars / 7 g protein / 4 g total fat / 2 g saturated fat / 357 mg sodium

WHOLE WHEAT PASTA WITH WALNUTS, SPINACH, AND MOZZARELLA

Your night-before-a-long-run pasta doesn't have to be drenched in tomato sauce. Walnuts add crunch and brain-healthy fats, while baby spinach is a quick way to add color, antioxidants, and folate to your dish.

MAKES 2 SERVINGS // TOTAL TIME: 15 MINUTES

1	tablespoon olive oil
½	cup walnut pieces
1	clove garlic, crushed
2	cups torn baby spinach leaves
1	teaspoon dried basil
	Salt and ground black pepper, to taste
4	ounces whole wheat spaghetti, cooked
2	tablespoons shredded part-skim mozzarella cheese

In a nonstick skillet over medium-low heat, heat the oil. Add the nuts and cook, stirring frequently, for 3 to 4 minutes. Add the garlic, spinach, basil, salt, and pepper. Cook, stirring frequently, for 3 to 5 minutes, or until the spinach wilts. Toss with the warm cooked pasta and top with the cheese.

NUTRITION PER SERVING

477 calories / 49 g carbohydrates / 10 g fiber / 2 g sugars / 15 g protein / 28 g total fat / 4 g saturated fat / 163 mg sodium

GRILLED EGGPLANT PARMESAN

When cooked just right, eggplant (covered in sauce and cheese!) is a great thing to sink your teeth into. The summer produce has antioxidants and B vitamins, and may even help promote brain health. For a little extra oomph (and to mirror a chicken Parm dish), coat the eggplant in whole wheat bread crumbs before cooking.

MAKES 4 SERVINGS // TOTAL TIME: 2 HOURS 20 MINUTES

FOR THE TOMATO SAUCE

- 2 teaspoons olive oil
- 1 large onion, chopped
- 3 cloves garlic, minced
- 4 pounds plum tomatoes, peeled and cut into chunks
- ½ cup chopped fresh basil
- ½ teaspoon salt

FOR THE EGGPLANT

- 2 medium eggplants, peeled and cut crosswise into ½"-thick slices
- 2 tablespoons olive oil
- 2 teaspoons dried Italian herb seasoning
  Salt and ground black pepper, to taste
- 1 cup shredded part-skim mozzarella cheese, divided
- 4 tablespoons grated Parmesan cheese, divided

TO MAKE THE TOMATO SAUCE: In a large, heavy saucepan over medium-high heat, heat the oil. Add the onion and garlic and cook, stirring, for 4 minutes, or until tender. Reduce the heat to low. Add the tomatoes and cook, stirring and breaking them up as they soften, for 45 minutes, or until thickened. Stir in the basil and salt.

TO MAKE THE EGGPLANT: Heat a grill or grill pan to medium-high and coat with olive oil spray. Brush the eggplant slices with the oil, sprinkle with the Italian seasoning, and season with salt and pepper. Grill the eggplant, in batches if necessary, turning once, for 8 minutes, or until tender and lightly browned.

Preheat the oven to 350°F. Arrange about 8 eggplant slices in a 13" × 9" baking dish. Sprinkle with ⅓ cup of the mozzarella and 1 tablespoon of the Parmesan. Spoon over ⅔ cup sauce and top with another layer of eggplant, ⅓ cup mozzarella, and 1 tablespoon Parmesan. Add ⅔ cup sauce and the remaining eggplant, ⅓ cup mozzarella, and 2 tablespoons Parmesan.

Cover the dish with foil and bake for 20 minutes, or until bubbling and heated through. Uncover and bake for 10 minutes, or until lightly browned on top.

NUTRITION PER SERVING

345 calories / 37 g carbohydrates / 12 g fiber / 21 g sugars / 16 g protein / 17 g total fat / 5.5 g saturated fat / 872 mg sodium

SMOKY BLACK BEAN GRILLED CHEESE

A simple grilled cheese is a runner staple for a quick protein- and carb-packed lunch. But you can easily up the nutritional ante by stuffing your sandwich with loads of tasty ingredients (we recommend keeping a fork on hand for spillage!). Black beans add a healthy dose of plant protein and fiber, while avocado boosts the sandwich's vitamin C and healthy fat.

MAKES 1 SERVING // TOTAL TIME: 15 MINUTES

2 slices whole grain bread

2 tablespoons black beans, mashed

1 jarred roasted red bell pepper, sliced

⅓ cup grated smoked Cheddar cheese

¼ avocado, thinly sliced

2 teaspoons unsalted butter

Top 1 slice of the bread with the black beans, roasted pepper, cheese, and avocado. Cover with the second bread slice.

In a skillet over medium-low heat, melt the butter. Add the sandwich and cook, turning once, until both sides are crispy and the cheese has melted.

NUTRITION PER SERVING   424 calories / 35 g carbohydrates / 9 g fiber / 5 g sugars / 18 g protein / 25 g total fat / 12 g saturated fat / 623 mg sodium

APPLE CHEDDAR GRILLED CHEESE

Just add apple and walnuts to your grilled cheese for a boost of fiber, antioxidants, and healthy fat. Serve this lunchtime favorite with a side of soup (see pages 180–199) for a hearty, nutrient-packed meal.

MAKES 1 SERVING // TOTAL TIME: 15 MINUTES

2   slices whole grain bread
¼   apple, thinly sliced
⅓   cup grated sharp Cheddar cheese
¼   teaspoon chopped fresh sage
1   tablespoon chopped walnuts
2   teaspoons unsalted butter

Top 1 slice of the bread with the apple, cheese, sage, and walnuts. Cover with the second bread slice.

In a skillet over medium-low heat, melt the butter. Add the sandwich and cook, turning once, until both sides are crispy and the cheese has melted.

NUTRITION PER SERVING 435 calories / 33 g carbohydrates / 6 g fiber / 9 g sugars / 17 g protein / 27 g total fat / 14 g saturated fat / 524 mg sodium

SMOKED CHILE AND TOMATO QUINOA

The spices are the star of this dish from chef duo Rich Landau and Kate Jacoby, who head up Vedge Restaurant in Philadelphia. Quinoa serves as the perfect vehicle for lycopene-packed tomatoes and exotic flavor.

MAKES 6 SERVINGS // TOTAL TIME: 30 MINUTES

1   **cup quinoa, rinsed**
1   **tablespoon olive oil**
¼   **cup finely chopped onion**
2   **cloves garlic, crushed**
6   **plum (Roma) tomatoes, chopped**
¼   **cup low-sodium vegetable broth, plus more if needed**
1   **teaspoon smoked paprika**
1   **teaspoon chipotle powder**
1   **teaspoon kosher salt**
1   **teaspoon ground black pepper**

Cook the quinoa according to the package directions.

Meanwhile, in a large skillet over medium heat, heat the oil. Add the onion and garlic and cook, stirring, for 5 minutes, or until the onion is translucent.

Stir in the tomatoes and cook, stirring, for 5 minutes, or until the tomatoes begin to break down. Pour in the vegetable broth, reduce the heat to medium-low, and bring to a simmer. Cook, stirring occasionally, for 5 minutes, or until the tomatoes completely break down into a sauce. Add additional broth, if needed, to reach a sauce consistency.

Add the paprika, chipotle powder, salt, and black pepper and stir to combine.

Fold the quinoa into the sauce and serve.

NUTRITION PER SERVING   144 calories / 22 g carbohydrates / 3 g fiber / 3 g sugars / 5 g protein / 4 g total fat / 1 g saturated fat / 351 mg sodium

SPICY THAI NOODLES

For a peanut-free Asian-inspired dish, look no further. Use whole wheat pasta to boost your fiber and protein (unless it's the night before a race—then use white pasta). Adjust the cayenne pepper to your liking; it gets hot quickly!

MAKES 8 SERVINGS // TOTAL TIME: 15 MINUTES, PLUS COOLING TIME

- 1 **pound angel hair pasta**
- ¼ **cup honey**
- ⅓ **cup soy sauce**
- ¼ **cup balsamic vinegar**
- ¼ **cup canola oil**
- 3 **tablespoons toasted sesame oil**
- 3 **tablespoons rice vinegar**
- 1 **tablespoon grated fresh ginger, or 1 teaspoon ground ginger**
- ¾ **teaspoon cayenne pepper, or more to taste**
- 3 **red bell peppers, thinly sliced**
- 1 **bunch scallions, thinly sliced**

Cook the pasta according to the package directions.

Meanwhile, in a large bowl, mix the honey, soy sauce, balsamic vinegar, canola oil, sesame oil, rice vinegar, ginger, and cayenne. Drain the pasta and toss together with the sauce and bell peppers.

Chill the noodles in the refrigerator, tossing occasionally, until cold. Sprinkle with the scallions and serve.

PRO TIP

Make it vegan by substituting agave nectar or brown rice syrup for the honey.

NUTRITION PER SERVING 380 calories / 55 g carbohydrates / 2 g fiber / 14 g sugars / 9 g protein / 13 g total fat / 1 g saturated fat / 592 mg sodium

COCONUT MILK RICE

Coconut milk is a unique and flavorful way to dress up any rice dish (and it makes black rice especially creamy). While it's high in saturated fat, coconut milk's medium-chain fatty acids are thought to be used by the body more quickly than other fats, making them less likely to be stored in your body. Add your favorite veggies (or tofu!) to this dish for a nutrient-packed meal.

MAKES 4 SERVINGS (OR 8 SERVINGS AS A SIDE) // TOTAL TIME: 40 MINUTES

- **1** can (13½ ounces) coconut milk
- **1⅔** cups water
- **1½** cups black or red rice
- **2** teaspoons toasted sesame oil
- **2** cups chopped pineapple
- **2** red or orange bell peppers, chopped
- **¼** cup salted peanuts
  Salt, to taste

In a large saucepan, combine the coconut milk, water, and rice. Bring to a boil, cover, and reduce the heat to low. Simmer until the rice is cooked, 35 to 45 minutes depending on the type of rice.

In a medium skillet over medium-high heat, heat the oil. Cook the pineapple and peppers for 5 minutes, or until tender. Stir in the peanuts until warmed. Toss with the rice. Sprinkle with salt to taste.

PRO TIP

An easy way to measure your rice, coconut milk, and water is with your coconut milk can: use 1 canful of each ingredient.

NUTRITION PER SERVING — 550 calories / 68 g carbohydrates / 7 g fiber / 6 g sugars / 12 g protein / 30 g total fat / 20 g saturated fat / 85 mg sodium

AVOCADO ENCHILADAS

This recipe was featured in the outtakes of the documentary *Spirit of the Marathon,* which chronicled six runners as they trained for and competed in the 2005 Chicago Marathon. "When the producer, Jon Dunham, was in my hometown of Mammoth Lakes, California, filming, I made him this dish knowing he was a vegetarian. And I'm Californian, so I have a few dishes in which avocados are the main attraction," says Olympic medalist Deena Kastor. Serve with a side of black beans for an extra boost of fiber and plant protein.

MAKES 10 SERVINGS // TOTAL TIME: 1 HOUR 30 MINUTES

FOR THE SAUCE

- 1 teaspoon canola oil
- ½ yellow onion, finely chopped
- ¼ cup ground cumin
- 3 tablespoons dried oregano
- 1 tablespoon sugar
- 2 cloves garlic, minced
- 1 can (28 ounces) crushed tomatoes
- 12 ounces beer
- 1 cup low-sodium vegetable broth or water

   Cayenne pepper, to taste

   Splash of balsamic vinegar

TO MAKE THE SAUCE: In a medium saucepan over medium heat, heat the oil. Add the onion and cook, stirring, for 5 minutes, or until softened. Add the cumin, oregano, sugar, and garlic and cook, stirring, for 2 minutes, or until fragrant. Stir in the tomatoes, beer, and broth or water and bring to a boil. Reduce the heat to a simmer and cook for 20 minutes, or until slightly thickened. Add cayenne pepper and balsamic vinegar to taste. You can keep the sauce thick and chunky or puree it in a blender.

PRO TIP

If you're on the run, instead of making your own sauce, combine a 28-ounce can of enchilada sauce and a 14-ounce can of crushed tomatoes.

(recipe continues)

NUTRITION PER SERVING   508 calories / 43 g carbohydrates / 16 g fiber / 7 g sugars / 13 g protein / 34 g total fat / 8 g saturated fat / 417 mg sodium

FOR THE ENCHILADAS

8   ripe avocados, pitted and peeled

1   cup fresh cilantro, coarsely chopped

½   red onion, chopped

1   jalapeño chile pepper, diced

    Juice of 1 lime

¾   teaspoon kosher salt

20 corn tortillas (6" diameter)

2   cups grated Monterey Jack cheese

TO MAKE THE ENCHILADAS: Meanwhile, preheat the oven to 400°F.

Chop the avocados. In a medium bowl, toss the avocados with the cilantro, red onion, jalapeño pepper, lime juice, and salt.

Spread ½ cup of the sauce on the bottom of a 13" × 9" baking dish. Dip a tortilla in the remaining sauce, spoon 2 heaping tablespoons of the avocado filling into the tortilla, and roll up. Repeat with the remaining tortillas, arranging them side by side, seam side down, in the baking dish. Pour the remaining sauce over the rolled tortillas. Sprinkle evenly with the cheese.

Cover with foil and bake for 25 minutes, or until hot. Remove the foil and bake for 5 minutes, or until the cheese bubbles and browns.

KOREAN GRILLED TOFU "STEAK"

One of the best things about tofu (besides its high protein content!) is its ability to take the flavor of whatever spices and sauces you cook it with. This dish, from chefs Rich Landau and Kate Jacoby, who co-own Vedge Restaurant in Philadelphia, has an authentic Korean barbecue taste, without the meat. Serve with a side of Sesame Bok Choy (see page 128) for an Asian-inspired dish that will fuel your runs and recovery.

MAKES 4 SERVINGS // TOTAL TIME: 20 MINUTES, PLUS 1 HOUR MARINATING TIME

FOR THE TOFU

- 1   block (12 to 14 ounces) extra-firm tofu, cut into 4 equal slabs
- ¼   cup reduced-sodium tamari or soy sauce
- ¼   cup canola oil
- 1   teaspoon white pepper

FOR THE SAUCE

- 2   tablespoons canola oil
- 2   tablespoons toasted sesame oil
- 2   tablespoons gochujang (red chile bean paste)
- 1   tablespoon finely chopped fresh ginger
- 1½ teaspoons brown sugar
- 1½ teaspoons water
- ½   teaspoon white pepper
- 1   clove garlic

TO MAKE THE TOFU: Place the tofu slabs in a baking dish. (For the best way to remove excess water from tofu, see the Pro Tip on page 147.) In a small bowl, whisk together the tamari or soy sauce, canola oil, and pepper. Pour the mixture over the tofu, turning the tofu a few times to coat. Cover and refrigerate for at least 1 hour or up to overnight.

Heat a grill to high heat. Brush and oil the grates.

TO MAKE THE SAUCE: In a blender, combine the canola oil, sesame oil, gochujang, ginger, sugar, water, pepper, and garlic. Blend until smooth.

Grill the tofu, turning once, for 6 minutes, or until good grill marks form. Be careful not to let it char too much.

Brush the top of the grilled tofu with the sauce and cook for 1 minute to let it absorb the flavors. Turn the tofu and brush with more sauce. Remove from the grill and serve with extra sauce drizzled on top.

NUTRITION PER SERVING

285 calories / 10 g carbohydrates / 2 g fiber / 5 g sugars / 11 g protein / 23 g total fat / 2.5 g saturated fat / 354 mg sodium

SPICY BLACK BEAN BURGERS

Beans provide plenty of recovery-friendly protein, fiber, and 10 percent of your iron needs per half cup. In order to absorb iron, pair your bean burger with foods that contain vitamin C, like pimiento peppers. While many veggie burgers use just bread crumbs to bind the patty together, this one adds ground walnuts, which are rich in heart-healthy omega-3 fatty acids and add a few extra grams of protein per burger.

MAKES 4 SERVINGS // TOTAL TIME: 20 MINUTES, PLUS 1 HOUR CHILLING TIME

½   **cup walnuts**

1   **small white onion, quartered**

1   **can (15½ ounces) black beans, drained and rinsed**

½   **cup whole wheat panko bread crumbs**

1   **teaspoon ground cumin**

1   **teaspoon chili powder**

½   **teaspoon smoked paprika**

½   **teaspoon kosher salt**

¼   **teaspoon ground black pepper**

1   **egg, lightly beaten**

1   **tablespoon canola oil**

4   **slices pepper Jack cheese**

4   **large soft pretzel rolls, sliced**

¼   **cup olive oil mayonnaise**

1   **teaspoon hot pepper sauce (optional)**

½   **cup sliced pimiento peppers, or 2 jarred roasted red bell pepper halves**

4   **lettuce leaves**

Place the walnuts in the bowl of a food processor. Process for 20 seconds, or until the nuts begin to resemble bread crumbs. Transfer to a medium bowl.

Add the onion to the food processor. Process for 10 seconds, or until finely chopped. Add half of the beans and process for 10 seconds, or until they're a chunky puree. Transfer the mixture to the bowl of walnuts. Add the remaining beans, bread crumbs, cumin, chili powder, paprika, salt, black pepper, and egg. Mix until well combined. With wet hands, form the mixture into 4 patties. Chill for 1 hour.

In a large nonstick skillet over medium-high heat, heat the oil. Add the patties and cook for 5 to 7 minutes, or until browned. Turn, top the patties with the cheese, and cook for 4 to 6 minutes, covering with a lid for the last few minutes to ensure the cheese melts.

Meanwhile, lightly toast the rolls. Spread 1½ teaspoons of the mayonnaise inside each top and bottom roll. Transfer the cooked patties to the bottom rolls. Top each patty with ¼ teaspoon of the hot pepper sauce (if using), one-quarter of the pimientos, and 1 lettuce leaf. Close with the top rolls.

NUTRITION PER SERVING

758 calories / 79 g carbohydrates / 11 g fiber / 7 g sugars / 27 g protein / 39 g total fat / 8 g saturated fat / 902 mg sodium

PUMPKIN CURRY WITH CUCUMBER RAITA

Nepalese-inspired veggie curry, or *takari*, is easier to digest than curry dishes with meat. Paired with a cucumber raita sauce, this dish will fuel your run and recovery, and help cool you off during those summer training months.

MAKES 2 SERVINGS // TOTAL TIME: 45 MINUTES

FOR THE CURRY

- 2 tablespoons coconut or olive oil
- 1 teaspoon cumin seeds
- 1 teaspoon fenugreek seeds
- ½ teaspoon mustard seeds
- 1 yellow onion, chopped
- 1 tablespoon minced garlic
- 1 Thai chile pepper or serrano pepper, seeded and finely chopped
- 1 teaspoon grated fresh ginger
- ¼ teaspoon kosher salt
- 2 pounds kabocha pumpkin or butternut squash, peeled, seeded, and cut into ¾" cubes (about 4 cups)
- ½ cup low-sodium vegetable broth
- 2 cups baby spinach leaves
- ¼ cup coconut water
- 1 tablespoon fresh lime juice

FOR THE RAITA

- ¾ cup fat-free plain Greek yogurt
- ½ cucumber, diced
- 1 tablespoon finely chopped fresh mint or cilantro leaves
- 1 tablespoon fresh lime juice
- ½ teaspoon minced garlic
- ¼ teaspoon kosher salt

- 2 pieces store-bought naan flatbread, warmed, for serving

TO MAKE THE CURRY: In a large skillet over medium heat, heat the oil. Add the cumin, fenugreek, and mustard seeds and cook for 4 minutes, or until the oil and seeds start to spatter. Add the onion, garlic, chile, ginger, and salt and cook, stirring frequently, for 4 minutes, or until softened and browned. Add the pumpkin or squash and the broth, bring to a simmer, reduce the heat, cover, and cook for 20 minutes, or until the pumpkin or squash is extremely soft. Uncover, increase the heat, and stir in the spinach, coconut water, and lime juice. Cook for 5 to 6 minutes, or until the spinach is wilted and the pan is nearly dry.

TO MAKE THE RAITA: Meanwhile, in a bowl or a blender, combine the yogurt, cucumber, mint or cilantro, lime juice, garlic, and salt. Stir or pulse to mix well. Serve the curry with the raita and warm naan.

NUTRITION PER SERVING

530 calories / 75 g carbohydrates / 10 g fiber / 18 g sugars / 22 g protein / 19 g total fat / 13 g saturated fat / 955 mg sodium

BAKED BLACK BEAN ROTINI

Yes, you *can* have healthy comfort food. Instead of traditional pasta, this black bean rotini adds extra protein and fiber to an otherwise wholly indulgent dish. Double the recipe if you're feeding a group of hungry runners after a long run. (Definitely don't eat this before you hit the road unless your stomach can handle lots of gooey cheese and fiber!)

MAKES 6 SERVINGS // TOTAL TIME: 50 MINUTES

12	**ounces black bean rotini**
1	**cup whole-milk ricotta**
⅔	**cup freshly grated Parmesan cheese**
2	**tablespoons chopped fresh basil**
2	**tablespoons chopped fresh parsley**
1	**teaspoon dried oregano**
¼	**teaspoon ground black pepper**
2	**cups chunky marinara sauce**
⅔	**cup freshly shredded mozzarella cheese, divided**

Preheat the oven to 350°F. Lightly oil an 8" × 8" baking dish.

Cook the pasta according to the package directions. Drain and rinse with cool water. In a large bowl, combine the ricotta, Parmesan, basil, parsley, oregano, and pepper. Add the cooked pasta, marinara sauce, and ⅓ cup of the mozzarella, tossing to distribute. Pour into the baking dish and top with the remaining ⅓ cup mozzarella. Bake, uncovered, for 20 minutes, or until browned and bubbling. Let rest for 5 minutes before serving.

NUTRITION PER SERVING 425 calories / 45 g carbohydrates / 12 g fiber / 7 g sugars / 29 g protein / 14 g total fat / 7 g saturated fat / 686 mg sodium

LENTIL SPAGHETTI WITH CREAMY PORCINI SAUCE

Lentil pasta is a sneaky way to boost your plant protein intake—and make your traditional spaghetti dishes more interesting. Mushrooms provide selenium and potassium, making this a nutrient powerhouse that tastes like it came out of an Italian grandmother's kitchen.

MAKES 6 SERVINGS // TOTAL TIME: 45 MINUTES

½ ounce dried porcini mushrooms

1 cup hot water (from tap)

1 pound lentil spaghetti

1 tablespoon olive oil

2 tablespoons unsalted butter

2 shallots, finely chopped

3 cloves garlic, minced

1 teaspoon fresh thyme leaves

2 cups half-and-half

   Kosher salt and ground black pepper, to taste

½ cup grated Parmesan cheese, divided

¼ cup chopped fresh parsley

In a medium bowl, soak the porcini in the hot water for 15 minutes, or until softened. Remove the mushrooms, squeezing to extract as much liquid as possible. Reserve the soaking water and coarsely chop the mushrooms. Set aside.

Cook the pasta according to the package directions. Reserve ¼ cup of the cooking water and drain. Set aside.

In a large skillet over medium heat, heat the oil and butter until the butter melts. Add the shallots and cook, stirring, for 2 minutes, or until translucent. Add the garlic and cook, stirring, for 30 seconds, or until fragrant. Add the mushrooms and the thyme and cook, stirring, for 2 minutes. Pour in the reserved mushroom soaking liquid, being careful to leave the sediment at the bottom of the bowl, and bring to a boil. Cook, stirring occasionally, for 2 minutes, or until the liquid is reduced slightly. Add the half-and-half and bring to a simmer. Cook, stirring occasionally, for 4 to 5 minutes, or until the half-and-half is reduced and thick. Season with salt and pepper.

Add the cooked pasta to the sauce, tossing well to coat and adding splashes of the reserved cooking water to loosen, if necessary. Add ¼ cup of the cheese and the parsley, toss, and remove from the heat.

Divide the pasta among 6 bowls, garnish with the remaining ¼ cup cheese, and serve immediately.

NUTRITION PER SERVING

504 calories / 62 g carbohydrates / 6 g fiber / 1 g sugars / 25 g protein / 19 g total fat / 10 g saturated fat / 302 mg sodium

6

SOUPS & STEWS

AVOCADO BASIL SOUP

Soup isn't just for chilly winter months. This cool variety will refresh you after a long run, and its avocado-and-kefir base promotes heart and gut health. Make a batch over the weekend and eat healthy lunches all week.

MAKES 6 SERVINGS // TOTAL TIME: 2 HOURS 10 MINUTES

1½ cups water

1½ cups plain kefir

2 small avocados

1 green bell pepper, chopped

½ English cucumber, chopped

1 cup fresh basil leaves

2 scallions, chopped

1 clove garlic, chopped

1 jalapeño chile pepper, seeded and chopped

Juice of ½ lime

½ teaspoon kosher salt

2 tablespoons olive oil

3 tablespoons roasted hulled pumpkin seeds

1 tablespoon chopped fresh chives

In a blender, combine the water, kefir, avocados, bell pepper, cucumber, basil, scallions, garlic, jalapeño pepper, lime juice, and salt. Blend until smooth. With the machine running on low speed, slowly drizzle in the oil. Chill for at least 2 hours. Sprinkle each serving with 1½ teaspoons pumpkin seeds and ½ teaspoon chives.

NUTRITION PER SERVING

182 calories / 10 g carbohydrates / 4 g fiber / 4 g sugars / 5 g protein / 15 g total fat / 3 g saturated fat / 205 mg sodium

FENNEL CAULIFLOWER CHOWDER

Cauliflower is all the rage right now: It's super versatile and high in vitamins C and K, and folate. Cauliflower makes for a healthy "chowdah" base, and the licorice-flavored fennel and potassium-rich potatoes really up the flavor and consistency of this dish. Serve with dunking bread for an extra carb boost before race day.

MAKES 6 SERVINGS // TOTAL TIME: 1 HOUR

1   tablespoon olive oil, plus more for drizzling

2   medium bulbs fennel, trimmed and diced

1   medium onion, diced

3   cloves garlic, minced

4   russet potatoes (about 2 pounds), diced

1   medium head cauliflower, cut into small florets (about 5 cups)

2   teaspoons poultry seasoning

1   teaspoon caraway seeds

½   teaspoon salt

6   cups low-sodium vegetable broth or water

⅓   cup sliced raw almonds

2½ tablespoons nutritional yeast

Red pepper flakes, for serving (optional)

Crusty bread, for serving (optional)

In a large saucepan over medium heat, heat the oil. Add the fennel and onion and cook, stirring, for 8 minutes, or until soft. Add the garlic and cook for 30 seconds, or until fragrant.

Stir in the potatoes, cauliflower, poultry seasoning, caraway, and salt. Pour in the vegetable broth or water. Bring to a boil, reduce the heat to a simmer, and cook for 30 minutes, or until the vegetables are completely tender.

Remove from the heat and let cool for 10 minutes. Pour half of the soup into a blender along with the almonds and nutritional yeast. Blend until smooth and stir back into the saucepan.

Serve drizzled with olive oil and sprinkled with red pepper flakes, with crusty bread on the side (if desired).

NUTRITION PER SERVING

349 calories / 62 g carbohydrates / 10 g fiber / 6 g sugars / 10 g protein / 8 g total fat / 1 g saturated fat / 384 mg sodium

PEANUT BUTTER SWEET POTATO SOUP

Perfect after a long, chilly run, this soup gets quality plant protein from peanut butter to help your body recover. The peanut butter is paired with sweet potato, so you'll get the carbs you need to refuel your muscles and get them ready for your next workout. Serve with a side of fresh greens or pour over wilted spinach.

MAKES 6 SERVINGS // TOTAL TIME: 55 MINUTES

1   tablespoon canola oil

1   yellow onion, finely chopped

4   cloves garlic, minced

2   tablespoons finely chopped fresh ginger

2   large sweet potatoes, peeled and cut into ½" dice (about 4 cups)

4   cups low-sodium vegetable broth

1   cup well-stirred canned unsweetened coconut milk

⅔   cup natural creamy peanut butter

½   teaspoon kosher salt, plus more to taste

Juice of 1 lime

In a large saucepan over low-medium heat, heat the oil until shimmering. Add the onion and cook, stirring frequently, for 5 minutes, or until translucent. Stir in the garlic and ginger and cook for 1 minute, or until fragrant.

Add the sweet potatoes and broth and bring to a boil. Reduce the heat to a simmer and cook for 20 to 25 minutes, or until the sweet potatoes are tender. Reduce the heat to very low.

In a bowl, whisk together the coconut milk, peanut butter, and salt. Stir the mixture into the soup and cook for 10 minutes to meld the flavors. (Do not let the soup boil, which can curdle the coconut milk.)

Add the lime juice and more salt to taste.

NUTRITION PER SERVING

376 calories / 30 g carbohydrates / 6 g fiber / 7 g sugars / 9 g protein / 25 g total fat / 9 g saturated fat / 415 mg sodium

VEGGIE CURRY STEW

Curry dishes may seem intimidating, but they don't have to be. This dish is not labor-intensive and can be on the table in less than 30 minutes. "During my buildup to the 2016 NYC Marathon, Sally Kipyego and her husband, Kevin Chelimo, stayed at my house in Flagstaff for two months. We did quite a bit of cooking together, and this is a recipe that was born during that time," says elite marathoner Matt Llano, who also served as a recipe tester for Shalane Flanagan and Elyse Kopecky's cookbook, *Run Fast. Eat Slow.* This stew is easily adaptable for those with allergies.

MAKES 6 SERVINGS // TOTAL TIME: 25 MINUTES

2   cups quinoa, rinsed

4   cups low-sodium vegetable broth

3   tablespoons olive oil

4   bell peppers, any color, chopped

1   sweet yellow onion, chopped

    Kosher salt and ground black pepper, to taste

3   cloves garlic, minced

1   can (15 ounces) unsweetened coconut milk, well stirred

2   tablespoons red curry paste

1   teaspoon grated fresh ginger

1   small bunch kale, chopped, or 4 cups chopped kale leaves

    Sliced avocado (optional)

In a medium pot over medium heat, combine the quinoa and broth and bring to a boil. Reduce the heat to a simmer, cover, and cook for 15 minutes, or until the quinoa is tender and the broth has been absorbed. Fluff with a fork and set aside.

Meanwhile, in a large skillet over medium heat, heat the oil. Add the bell peppers, onion, and a pinch of salt and black pepper and cook, stirring, for 5 to 7 minutes, or until the vegetables are softened and slightly translucent. Stir in the garlic and cook for 30 seconds, or until fragrant. Add the coconut milk, curry paste, and ginger. Reduce the heat to a simmer, add the kale, and cook for 3 to 5 minutes, or until wilted. Season with additional salt and black pepper.

To serve, divide the quinoa among 6 bowls and top with the curry stew and avocado, if desired.

NUTRITION PER SERVING

496 calories / 55 g carbohydrates / 8 g fiber / 10 g sugars / 13 g protein / 26 g total fat / 15 g saturated fat / 400 mg sodium

COCONUT CURRY LENTIL SOUP

This mineral-rich, immune-boosting soup is loaded with nutrient-dense whole foods. "My family calls this the 'superfoods soup,'" says Elyse Kopecky, coauthor of the cookbook *Run Fast. Eat Slow.* In fact, Elyse's coauthor, Shalane Flanagan, lived on this soup while training for the 2017 New York City Marathon, which she won. Coconut milk, garlic, and onions are natural antivirals to help fight off the common cold. Freeze individual portions for quick weeknight meals when you're feeling sniffly or when training leaves you short on time to cook. Leftovers are also great served over brown rice.

MAKES 8 SERVINGS // TOTAL TIME: 1 HOUR

2	tablespoons extra-virgin olive oil
3	carrots, chopped
3	ribs celery, chopped
1	yellow onion, chopped
2	teaspoons fine sea salt
2	tablespoons curry powder
4	cloves garlic, minced
6	cups water
1	can (13½ ounces) unsweetened coconut milk
1	can (14½ ounces) diced tomatoes
1	sweet potato, chopped
1	cup green lentils
3	cups chopped kale
1	to 2 tablespoons fresh lime juice (optional)

In a large pot over medium heat, heat the oil. Add the carrots, celery, onion, and salt and cook, stirring occasionally, for 5 minutes, or until softened but not brown. Add the curry powder and garlic and cook, stirring, for 30 seconds, or until fragrant, being careful not to let the spices brown.

Add the water, coconut milk, tomatoes, sweet potato, and lentils. Bring to a boil, reduce the heat, and simmer, covered, stirring occasionally, for 30 minutes, or until the lentils are soft. Stir in the kale and simmer for 5 minutes, or until wilted. If too thick, thin with additional water. Remove from the heat and stir in the lime juice, if using.

NUTRITION PER SERVING

264 calories / 28 g carbohydrates / 7 g fiber / 5 g sugars / 8 g protein / 15 g total fat / 10 g saturated fat / 570 mg sodium

BUTTERNUT SQUASH SOUP

When you're in search of quality comfort food, this one-pot soup won't disappoint. The coconut milk gives the soup a luxurious and creamy consistency that complements the sweetness of the squash. Not to mention, butternut squash is a runner superfood: It's packed with vitamin A and potassium.

MAKES 6 SERVINGS // TOTAL TIME: 1 HOUR 45 MINUTES

- 1 **butternut squash, cut into quarters lengthwise (with seeds and skin intact)**
- 1 **tablespoon coconut oil**
- 1 **large yellow onion, sliced**
- 1 **teaspoon ground cinnamon**
- ¼ **teaspoon ground allspice**
- 1 **bay leaf**
- 1½ **teaspoons kosher salt, divided**
- 1 **tablespoon maple syrup**
- 4 **to 5 cups boiling water**
- 1 **can (13½ ounces) unsweetened coconut milk**

Preheat the oven to 425°F.

Line a baking sheet with parchment paper and place the butternut squash on the sheet, flesh side down. Roast for 1 hour, or until soft. (Check at 45 minutes.) Allow the squash to cool slightly until it can be handled. Remove the seeds and discard. Carefully scoop out the roasted flesh and reserve in a bowl. Discard the skins.

Meanwhile, in a large, heavy-bottomed pot over medium heat, heat the oil. Add the onion, cinnamon, allspice, bay leaf, and ½ teaspoon of the salt. Cook for 15 minutes, or until the onion is soft and translucent. Reduce the heat if the onion is browning too quickly.

Add the maple syrup and the roasted squash. Add the boiling water, enough to completely cover the squash mixture by about 1". Add the remaining 1 teaspoon salt, stir to combine, and bring to a boil.

Reduce the heat to a simmer and cook for 30 minutes, uncovered. Stir occasionally, tasting and adjusting the seasoning if needed. The soup should be thick.

Add the coconut milk, stir to combine, and turn off the heat. Carefully remove the bay leaf with a spoon and discard. Transfer the soup, in batches, to a blender and process until smooth. The consistency should be silky and creamy.

NUTRITION PER SERVING

242 calories / 31 g carbohydrates / 8 g fiber / 9 g sugars / 3 g protein / 14 g total fat / 11.5 g saturated fat / 511 mg sodium

CHICKPEA PESTO TOMATO SOUP

Chickpeas give the classic tomato soup a health (and taste!) upgrade. Research shows that people who eat half a cup of fiber-rich chickpeas a day tend to eat less junk food and feel full after a meal compared to those who don't.

MAKES 4 SERVINGS // TOTAL TIME: 30 MINUTES

- 1 tablespoon extra-virgin olive oil
- 1 onion, chopped
- 2 cloves garlic, minced
- 1 can (28 ounces) fire-roasted crushed tomatoes
- 2 cups low-sodium vegetable broth
- 1 teaspoon sugar
- ¼ teaspoon ground black pepper, plus more as needed
- 1 can (15 ounces) chickpeas, rinsed and drained
- 4 tablespoons basil pesto (jarred or homemade)

In a large soup pot over medium heat, heat the oil. Add the onion and cook, stirring frequently, for 4 minutes, or until soft. Add the garlic and cook, stirring frequently, for 30 seconds, or until fragrant. Add the tomatoes and broth. Increase the heat to high and bring the soup to a boil. Reduce the heat to low and simmer for 5 minutes. Add the sugar and pepper.

If you prefer a smooth texture, transfer the mixture to a blender and puree until smooth. Transfer the soup back to the pot. If you prefer a chunky texture, skip this step.

Add the chickpeas to the pot. Cover with a lid and simmer for 10 minutes. Season with more pepper, if desired. Ladle the soup into 4 bowls and top each with 1 tablespoon pesto.

NUTRITION PER SERVING

237 calories / 32 g carbohydrates / 7 g fiber / 12.5 g sugars / 8 g protein / 10 g total fat / 1.5 g saturated fat / 932 mg sodium

HEIRLOOM TOMATO GAZPACHO

Best made at the height of tomato season, this cold tomato soup is light, refreshing, and delicious any time of day. Try to use the freshest tomatoes, cucumber, and basil because this dish relies on the quality of the ingredients. Extra-virgin olive oil balances the vibrant flavor of the tomatoes and gives the soup a silky texture. The sherry vinegar is worth seeking out as it adds a nice, sweet acidity. It may be hard to wait for the soup to chill, but it's definitely worth it—the gazpacho will taste even better cold. It's packed with nutrients and a great way to cool off after a hot run.

MAKES 4 SERVINGS // TOTAL TIME: 10 MINUTES, PLUS 3 HOURS CHILLING TIME

- 2 pounds heirloom tomatoes, cored, seeded, and quartered
- ½ large cucumber, peeled and chopped, plus more for garnish
- 1 clove garlic, minced
- 3 tablespoons sherry vinegar or red wine vinegar
- ½ cup extra-virgin olive oil, plus more for garnish
- 1 teaspoon red pepper flakes
- 1 teaspoon sea salt, plus more to taste
- 1 cup fresh basil leaves

In a blender, combine the tomatoes, cucumber, and garlic. Blend until smooth.

Add the vinegar, oil, red pepper flakes, and salt and blend again until incorporated and emulsified. Add the basil leaves and blend until the soup has a silky texture. Taste and adjust the seasonings as needed. For a very smooth soup, pass through a fine-mesh sieve or food mill, if desired.

Cover and refrigerate for at least 3 hours. To serve, stir the soup, then ladle into 4 bowls. Top with a drizzle of olive oil and a sprinkle of chopped cucumber.

NUTRITION PER SERVING

291 calories / 10 g carbohydrates / 3 g fiber / 7 g sugars / 2 g protein / 29 g total fat / 4 g saturated fat / 407 mg sodium

THAI CARROT SOUP

This cool soup has a warming sensation thanks to the Thai-influenced inclusion of ginger and lime. The carrots are an excellent source of beta-carotene—a precursor to vitamin A—to boost your immune system.

MAKES 4 SERVINGS // TOTAL TIME: 50 MINUTES, PLUS 2 HOURS CHILLING TIME

1   pound carrots, chopped
1   orange bell pepper, quartered
2   shallots, peeled (left whole)
4   cloves garlic, peeled (left whole)
1   tablespoon olive oil
1   cup low-sodium vegetable broth
1   can (13½ ounces) light coconut milk
1   piece (1") fresh ginger, peeled
1   tablespoon honey or agave nectar
    Juice of 1 lime
2   teaspoons curry powder
¼   teaspoon salt
4   teaspoons chopped unsalted roasted peanuts
4   teaspoons fresh cilantro

Preheat the oven to 400°F. On a baking sheet, toss the carrots, pepper, shallots, and garlic with the oil. Roast for 30 minutes, or until the vegetables have browned and are tender. Let cool for 10 minutes.

Transfer the vegetables to a blender and add the broth, coconut milk, ginger, honey or agave, lime juice, curry powder, and salt. Blend until smooth. Chill for at least 2 hours. Serve each portion topped with 1 teaspoon peanuts and 1 teaspoon cilantro.

To make the soup vegan, use agave nectar instead of honey.

NUTRITION PER SERVING

242 calories / 31 g carbohydrates / 4 g fiber / 14 g sugars / 5 g protein / 12 g total fat / 6 g saturated fat / 286 mg sodium

VEGGIE STEW WITH CHEESY BREADSTICKS

You definitely don't need meat to make a hearty, nutritious, delicious stew. This veggie-packed version will warm you up after a cold run and help you refuel with protein. Pair with cheesy breadsticks and come back for seconds (and maybe thirds).

MAKES 6 SERVINGS // TOTAL TIME: 4 HOURS 15 MINUTES

FOR THE STEW

- 1   can (28 ounces) no-salt-added diced tomatoes
- 1   can (15 ounces) no-salt-added red kidney beans
- 1   can (15 ounces) no-salt-added pinto beans
- 2   small zucchini, chopped
- 1   medium onion, chopped
- 1   green bell pepper, chopped
- 2   ribs celery, chopped
- 1   large carrot, shredded
- 1   can (4 ounces) chopped green chilies
- 1   teaspoon chili powder
- 1   teaspoon kosher salt
- ½   teaspoon dried oregano
- ¼   teaspoon crushed red pepper flakes
- 2   scallions, thinly sliced

FOR THE BREADSTICKS

- 1   ball (18 to 22 ounces) pizza dough (refrigerated or thawed from frozen)
- 1   tablespoon olive oil
- 1   cup shredded Cheddar cheese, divided

TO MAKE THE STEW: In a 6-quart slow cooker, stir together the tomatoes (with juice), beans with liquid, zucchini, onion, bell pepper, celery, carrot, green chilies with liquid, chili powder, salt, oregano, and red pepper flakes. Cover and cook for 4 hours on high or 6 hours on low, or until the vegetables are tender.

TO MAKE THE BREADSTICKS: Preheat the oven to 400°F. Spray a baking sheet with cooking spray.

On a lightly floured surface, roll the pizza dough into a ¼"-thick rectangle. Brush with the oil and sprinkle ½ cup of the cheese over the top, pressing lightly so the cheese sticks to the dough. Cut the dough into twelve ½"-wide strips, twist each strip a few times, and place 1" apart on the baking sheet. Sprinkle the remaining ½ cup cheese on top and bake for 15 minutes, or until golden brown. Remove from the oven and cool on a wire rack.

To serve, divide the stew among 6 bowls, sprinkle with the scallions, and serve with the breadsticks.

NUTRITION PER SERVING   456 calories / 74 g carbohydrates / 11 g fiber / 11 g sugars / 20 g protein / 10 g total fat / 4 g saturated fat / 1,045 mg sodium

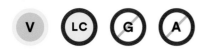

RED LENTIL AND BLACK BEAN STEW

Beans and lentils create a thick stew that will fill you up and keep you feeling full, thanks to protein and fiber. Chili powder, cumin, and paprika add a nice flavor and anti-inflammatory antioxidants to help fight running-related inflammation. Can't find red lentils? Any color will work.

MAKES 4 SERVINGS // TOTAL TIME: 45 MINUTES

1 tablespoon extra-virgin olive oil

1 onion, chopped

2 cloves garlic, minced

½ teaspoon chili powder

½ teaspoon ground cumin

¼ teaspoon paprika

4 cups low-sodium vegetable broth

1 tablespoon tomato paste

¾ cup red lentils

1 can (15 ounces) black beans, rinsed and drained, half of the beans mashed with a fork

Juice of 1 lime

¼ teaspoon salt

¼ teaspoon ground black pepper

2 tablespoons chopped fresh cilantro

In a large soup pot over medium heat, heat the oil. Add the onion and cook, stirring frequently, for 5 minutes, or until soft. Add the garlic, chili powder, cumin, and paprika and cook for 1 minute. Add the broth and tomato paste and stir to combine.

Increase the heat to high and bring the mixture to a boil. Add the lentils. Reduce the heat to a simmer and cook for 25 minutes, or until the lentils are tender. Add the black beans (whole and mashed), lime juice, salt, and pepper. Cook for 5 minutes, or until heated through. Ladle into bowls and sprinkle with the cilantro.

NUTRITION PER SERVING · 396 calories / 39 g carbohydrates / 10 g fiber / 5 g sugars / 14 g protein / 5 g total fat / 0.5 g saturated fat / 537 mg sodium

BLACK AND WHITE BEAN SOUP

Fill up on two types of beans in this soup, which can be stored in the refrigerator for up to 5 days. Or make a double batch and freeze for up to 3 months for a quick lunch or dinner. For a little Southwestern fire, try adding minced jalapeño peppers or reconstituted dried chipotle peppers.

MAKES 8 SERVINGS // TOTAL TIME: 40 MINUTES

- 1 tablespoon olive oil
- 1 cup chopped onions
- 1 cup chopped red and green bell peppers
- ½ cup sliced carrots
- 1½ teaspoons chopped garlic
- 4 cups low-sodium vegetable broth, divided
- 1 cup canned black beans, rinsed and drained
- 1 cup canned cannellini beans, rinsed and drained
- 1 cup frozen corn kernels
- 1 teaspoon ground cumin
- 1 teaspoon ground coriander
- 1 tablespoon chopped fresh flat-leaf parsley

In a large saucepan over medium heat, heat the oil. Add the onions and cook for 5 minutes, or until soft. Add the bell peppers, carrots, garlic, and ½ cup of the broth. Cook, stirring often, for 10 minutes. Add the black beans, cannellini beans, corn, cumin, coriander, and the remaining 3½ cups broth. Simmer for 15 to 20 minutes, or until the vegetables are tender. Stir in the parsley before serving.

NUTRITION PER SERVING

108 calories / 19 g carbohydrates / 5 g fiber / 4 g sugars / 5 g protein / 2 g total fat / 0 g saturated fat / 403 mg sodium

BLACK BEAN AND SWEET POTATO CHILI

This chili is hearty and filling with plenty of plant protein. And unlike most vegetarian chilis that have wheat, dairy, or soy, this one is vegan and can be allergen-free if you use avocado or olive oil. Black beans are high in antioxidants, fiber, and protein, while providing a great texture and base. If you're into cheese, top with a sprinkling of Cheddar.

MAKES 6 SERVINGS // TOTAL TIME: 1 HOUR

1 tablespoon coconut oil

1 large sweet potato, diced

1 large onion, diced

1 red bell pepper, diced

2 carrots, diced

3 ribs celery, diced

1 jalapeño chile pepper, diced

1½ teaspoons salt, divided

3 tablespoons ancho chili powder

1 tablespoon ground cumin

1 tablespoon ground coriander

1 tablespoon dried oregano

2 cloves garlic, minced

½ teaspoon ground cinnamon

½ teaspoon ground ginger

1 can (28 ounces) crushed fire-roasted tomatoes

2 tablespoons tomato paste

2 cans (15 ounces each) no-salt-added organic black beans, rinsed and drained

1 can (4 ounces) diced green chilies

1 cup water

1 avocado, diced, for serving

In a heavy-bottomed 6- to 8-quart pot over medium heat, heat the oil. Add the sweet potato, onion, bell pepper, carrots, celery, jalapeño pepper, and ½ teaspoon of the salt. Cook, stirring, for 8 minutes, or until the onion is translucent.

Stir in the chili powder, cumin, coriander, oregano, garlic, cinnamon, and ginger. Add the tomatoes and tomato paste and cook for 2 minutes.

Stir in the black beans, green chilies, water, and the remaining 1 teaspoon salt. Bring to a boil, reduce the heat to low, cover, and simmer, stirring occasionally, for 30 minutes, or until the flavors have melded. Uncover and simmer for 10 minutes, or until the chili thickens. Season with additional salt, if needed, and serve in deep bowls. Top with the avocado.

NUTRITION PER SERVING 294 calories / 52 g carbohydrates / 13 g fiber / 14 g sugars / 11 g protein / 7 g total fat / 2.5 g saturated fat / 968 mg sodium

7 SALADS

KALE FARRO SALAD WITH LEMON-MISO DRESSING

This salad sparked the idea for *Run Fast. Eat Slow.*, the *New York Times* bestseller cowritten by Olympic medalist and 2017 New York City Marathon winner Shalane Flanagan and chef runner Elyse Kopecky. Raw spinach, while chock-full of vitamins and minerals like vitamin C and iron, can interfere with the absorption of some minerals, which drove the pair to try a kale-based salad. Farro adds healthy carbohydrates, and the dressing has immune benefits thanks to the garlic.

MAKES 8 SERVINGS // TOTAL TIME: 45 MINUTES

FOR THE SALAD

1   **cup farro, rinsed and drained**

1   **cup chopped walnuts**

1   **large bunch kale leaves, stems removed, finely chopped**

1   **small head radicchio, quartered, cored, and cut crosswise into thin strips**

1   **cup grated Parmesan cheese**

FOR THE DRESSING

⅓   **cup fresh lemon juice**

3   **cloves garlic, minced**

2   **teaspoons miso paste (preferably mellow white)**

½   **teaspoon fine sea salt**

¼   **teaspoon ground black pepper**

½   **cup extra-virgin olive oil**

Place the farro in a large pot and add enough water to cover by a couple of inches. Bring to a boil over high heat. Reduce the heat to low and simmer, covered, for 30 minutes, or until the farro is tender but still chewy. Drain the farro and set aside to cool.

Meanwhile, in a medium skillet over medium heat, toast the walnuts for 8 minutes, or until just fragrant and just taking on color. Set aside.

TO MAKE THE DRESSING: In a bowl, whisk together the lemon juice, garlic, miso, salt, and pepper until well mixed. Slowly stream in the oil, whisking constantly, until the dressing is emulsified.

TO ASSEMBLE THE SALAD: In a large salad bowl, toss the kale with three-quarters of the dressing. Gently massage the kale with the dressing for 5 minutes to soften the leaves. Add the radicchio, cheese, walnuts, and farro to the kale and toss again. Taste and add the remaining dressing, if needed. This salad can be made in advance—it tastes even better the next day. Cover and refrigerate leftovers for up to 5 days. Any remaining dressing will keep in the fridge for up to 1 week.

NUTRITION PER SERVING

360 calories / 22 g carbohydrates / 3 g fiber / 1 g sugars / 11 g protein / 27 g total fat / 4.5 g saturated fat / 336 mg sodium

CLASSIC WINTER KALE SALAD

This salad is actually good any time of the year, and it's even better when it sits overnight, which helps soften the kale, says Chris Mosier, the first known transgender athlete to represent a US men's team in international competition. This leafy green is all the rage right now, thanks to its sky-high levels of vitamins A and C. If you need a boost of complex carbs, add a cup of cooked grains, like quinoa or farro, and toss.

MAKES 4 SERVINGS // TOTAL TIME: 10 MINUTES

2	large bunches kale (any variety)
3	tablespoons olive oil
	Sea salt, to taste
2	carrots, grated
½	cup raisins
½	cup finely chopped red onion
	Juice of 1 lemon

Wash, stem, and chop the kale into bite-size pieces. Place the kale in a large bowl and add the oil and a pinch of salt. Massage the kale with the oil for 5 to 10 minutes, or until it begins to soften. The amount of kale will look significantly smaller when done.

Toss in the carrots, raisins, onion, and lemon juice. Season with more salt.

NUTRITION PER SERVING 195 calories / 25 g carbohydrates / 3 g fiber / 13 g sugars / 4 g protein / 11 g total fat / 1.5 g saturated fat / 147 mg sodium

CAPRESE FARRO SALAD

This recipe takes the traditional Caprese salad—fresh mozzarella, tomatoes, and basil—and boosts its nutrition with farro, a chewy, nutty-flavored whole grain that's a good source of protein and fiber. Serve as a meal or take a smaller portion as a side.

MAKES 4 SERVINGS // TOTAL TIME: 35 MINUTES

- 1½ cups farro (about 10 ounces)
- 1 teaspoon kosher salt
- 8 ounces cherry tomatoes, halved
- 8 ounces fresh mozzarella, cubed, or 8 ounces mini mozzarella balls
- ½ cup thinly sliced fresh basil
- ¼ cup extra-virgin olive oil
- 2½ tablespoons balsamic vinegar
- 1 teaspoon agave nectar or honey
- Ground black pepper, to taste

Cook the farro according to the package directions with the salt. Drain well and transfer to a large bowl.

Add the tomatoes, mozzarella, and basil. Toss to combine.

In a small bowl, whisk together the oil, vinegar, agave nectar or honey, and pepper to taste. Drizzle over the farro mixture and toss to coat. Serve immediately, or let cool and serve at room temperature.

PRO TIP

Shalane Flanagan and Elyse Kopecky's favorite farro is Bob's Red Mill organic farro, which cooks more quickly without compromising flavor or nutrition like some other quick-cooking farro.

NUTRITION PER SERVING   550 calories / 55 g carbohydrates / 5 g fiber / 4 g sugars / 20 g protein / 27 g total fat / 10 g saturated fat / 563 mg sodium

QUINOA FRUIT SALAD WITH MAPLE DRESSING

Made up of beige, red, and black grains, tricolored South American quinoa packs a bigger antioxidant punch that may help improve recovery from training. Fruits add an extra layer of antioxidant protection to this naturally sweetened salad. Mix in nutty hemp seeds, and you'll get a boost of protein and heart-healthy omega fats.

MAKES 6 SERVINGS // TOTAL TIME: 25 MINUTES

FOR THE SALAD

- ¾ **cup tricolored quinoa, rinsed**
- 1½ **cups water**
- 2 **cups blackberries or blueberries**
- 2 **cups diced pineapple**
- ½ **cup dried tart cherries**
- ⅓ **cup coconut chips**
- ⅓ **cup unsalted shelled pistachios**
- ⅓ **cup sliced fresh mint**
- 3 **tablespoons hemp seeds (hemp hearts)**

FOR THE DRESSING

- 2 **tablespoons pure maple syrup**
- 1 **teaspoon grated lime zest Juice of ½ lime**
- ½ **teaspoon ground ginger**
- ¼ **teaspoon salt**

In a saucepan, combine the quinoa and water and bring to a boil. Reduce the heat and simmer, covered, for 12 minutes, or until the grains are tender and the water has been absorbed. Set aside, covered, for 5 minutes, then fluff with a fork.

TO MAKE THE DRESSING: Meanwhile, in a small bowl, whisk together the maple syrup, lime zest, lime juice, ginger, and salt.

TO ASSEMBLE THE SALAD: Place the quinoa in a large bowl and toss with the blackberries or blueberries, pineapple, cherries, coconut chips, pistachios, mint, and hemp. Toss the dressing with the quinoa salad and serve.

SALADS

NUTRITION PER SERVING	273 calories / 43 g carbohydrates / 9 g fiber / 19 g sugars / 8 g protein / 9 g total fat / 0.5 g saturated fat / 104 mg sodium

WATERMELON, GINGER, AND CUCUMBER SALAD

Perfect for a summer picnic, this salad will help you hydrate before a hot run (and it's super refreshing after one!). Watermelon is also an excellent source of the electrolyte potassium, which helps maintain muscle function. The ginger and jalapeño give this dish a little kick, which actually may help your body cool off.

MAKES 4 SERVINGS // TOTAL TIME: 15 MINUTES

4 cups cubed (1" pieces) watermelon

2 cups diced seedless cucumber

2 tablespoons finely chopped fresh ginger

2 tablespoons chopped fresh cilantro

1 jalapeño chile pepper, seeded and chopped (optional)

Grated zest and juice of 1 lime

⅛ teaspoon salt

1 avocado, diced

In a large bowl, combine the watermelon, cucumber, ginger, cilantro, jalapeño pepper (if using), lime zest and juice, and salt. Add the avocado when ready to serve.

NUTRITION PER SERVING

141 calories / 20 g carbohydrates / 5 g fiber / 11 g sugars / 2 g protein / 8 g total fat / 1 g saturated fat / 80 mg sodium

ROASTED ROOT VEGETABLE SALAD WITH LEMON-DIJON VINAIGRETTE

Warm up and add a dose of healthy complex carbohydrates to your meal with this salad. Roasting brings out the natural sugars in vegetables, giving them great flavor without the need for sugar or much salt. Make this a vegan favorite by cutting out the feta.

MAKES 4 SERVINGS // TOTAL TIME: 45 MINUTES

FOR THE SALAD

- 6 baby carrots, cut into matchsticks
- 6 small red potatoes, halved
- 3 parsnips, cut into matchsticks
- 4 shallots, halved
- 1 tablespoon olive oil
- 3 cups arugula
- ½ teaspoon salt
- ¼ teaspoon ground black pepper
- ½ cup crumbled feta cheese

FOR THE VINAIGRETTE

- 2 tablespoons fresh lemon juice
- 1 tablespoon white wine vinegar
- 2 teaspoons Dijon mustard
- ¼ teaspoon kosher salt
- ¼ teaspoon ground black pepper
- ¼ cup + 2 tablespoons extra-virgin olive oil

TO MAKE THE SALAD: Preheat the oven to 425°F. On a rimmed baking sheet, toss the carrots, potatoes, parsnips, and shallots with the oil. Roast for 30 minutes, or until tender. Let cool to room temperature.

TO MAKE THE DRESSING: In a small bowl, whisk together the lemon juice, vinegar, mustard, salt, and pepper. Slowly whisk in the oil in a steady stream.

In a salad bowl, toss the arugula and root vegetables with the dressing. Season with the salt and pepper. Serve sprinkled with the cheese.

NUTRITION PER SERVING	593 calories / 78 g carbohydrates / 9 g fiber / 13 g sugars / 12 g protein / 28 g total fat / 6 g saturated fat / 731 mg sodium

SPINACH, BERRY, AND GOAT CHEESE SALAD

Fill up on protein from goat cheese and healthy fat from walnuts, which are also one of the best foods for brain health. The fat in this salad, which makes it hearty enough to serve as a meal, will also help your body absorb the vitamin K found in spinach.

MAKES 2 SERVINGS // TOTAL TIME: 10 MINUTES

¼ **cup walnut halves**

1½ **tablespoons extra-virgin olive oil**

1½ **tablespoons red wine vinegar**

2 **teaspoons blackstrap molasses**

Grated zest of ½ lemon

¼ **teaspoon grated fresh ginger**

6 **cups baby spinach**

1 **cup sliced strawberries**

½ **cup blueberries**

4 **ounces goat cheese**

Ground black pepper, to taste

In a small dry skillet over medium heat, toast the walnuts for 8 minutes, or until fragrant and just beginning to take on color.

Meanwhile, in a small bowl, whisk together the oil, vinegar, molasses, lemon zest, and ginger. Set aside.

In a large bowl, combine the spinach, strawberries, and blueberries and toss gently. Pour the dressing over the salad and toss gently to coat the spinach leaves.

Divide the salad between 2 plates or bowls. Top each serving with half of the walnuts, 2 ounces of the cheese, and black pepper.

NUTRITION PER SERVING

479 calories / 27 g carbohydrates / 7 g fiber / 13 g sugars / 17 g protein / 36 g total fat / 14 g saturated fat / 413 mg sodium

CHICKPEA TABBOULEH SALAD

Traditional tabbouleh is basically a fresh-herb salad sprinkled with bulgur wheat. This version swaps the bulgur for ready-made chickpeas, which gets this salad to the table in no time. Not to mention, chickpeas are high in fiber and protein and can help stabilize blood sugar levels.

MAKES 4 SERVINGS // TOTAL TIME: 10 MINUTES

- 2 cans (15 ounces each) chickpeas, rinsed and drained
- 1 cup packed fresh flat-leaf parsley, finely chopped
- 1 cup packed fresh basil leaves, finely chopped
- 2 cloves garlic, minced
  Grated zest and juice of 1 lemon
- 2 tablespoons olive oil
- ½ teaspoon kosher salt, plus more to taste
- ¼ teaspoon ground black pepper, plus more to taste
- ½ cup freshly grated Parmesan cheese

In a large bowl, combine the chickpeas, parsley, basil, garlic, 1 teaspoon of the lemon zest, the lemon juice, oil, salt, and pepper. Gently toss until well mixed. Add the cheese and stir to combine. Taste and adjust the seasoning with the lemon zest, salt, and pepper, if necessary. Serve immediately, or set aside, or chill, covered, for a couple of hours.

PRO TIP

Prepare the salad before you start making the rest of your meal to give the flavors time to meld.

NUTRITION PER SERVING

249 calories / 21 g carbohydrates / 6 g fiber / 0 g sugars / 13 g protein / 14 g total fat / 3 g saturated fat / 877 mg sodium

WATERCRESS AND RADICCHIO SALAD WITH MUSTARD VINAIGRETTE

This light and refreshing salad is a great side to any summer barbecue meal. Watercress is one of the best sources of vitamin K, which promotes bone health and maintenance and aids in blood clotting. To make this dish vegan, use agave nectar instead of honey.

MAKES 6 SERVINGS // TOTAL TIME: 15 MINUTES

¼ **cup sliced almonds**

2 **tablespoons red or white wine vinegar**

1 **tablespoon honey or agave nectar**

1 **tablespoon Dijon mustard**

½ **teaspoon minced garlic**

¼ **cup + 2 tablespoons olive oil**

Salt and ground black pepper, to taste

6 **cups lightly packed watercress, tough stems removed**

3 **cups lightly packed radicchio leaves, torn**

In a small dry skillet over medium heat, toast the almonds for 5 minutes, or until fragrant and just beginning to take on color.

In a large bowl, whisk together the vinegar, honey or agave, mustard, and garlic. Add the oil in a stream, whisking. Season with salt and pepper. Add the watercress and radicchio and toss to coat. Divide the greens among 6 salad plates and top each with 2 teaspoons of the almonds.

NUTRITION PER SERVING

248 calories / 8 g carbohydrates / 1 g fiber / 5 g sugars / 3 g protein / 23 g total fat / 3 g saturated fat / 119 mg sodium

GREENS AND COUSCOUS SALAD

Whole wheat couscous is a filling, runner-friendly grain that will ramp up any salad. It's also a nice break from traditional pasta for a carb load. This recipe calls for low-fat yogurt but can be made with full-fat yogurt to better stave off hunger.

MAKES 1 SERVING // TOTAL TIME: 10 MINUTES

- 2 cups spinach or beet greens
- 2 cloves garlic, minced
- ¾ cup cooked whole wheat couscous
- ¼ cup low-fat plain yogurt
- ½ teaspoon ground cumin
- 1 teaspoon fresh lemon juice
- 2 tablespoons pine nuts

In a nonstick skillet over medium heat, cook the spinach or beet greens with the garlic for 2 to 3 minutes, or until the greens are wilted. Combine the cooked greens with the couscous.

In a medium bowl, combine the yogurt, cumin, and lemon juice. Add the greens and couscous and toss. Sprinkle with the pine nuts.

NUTRITION PER SERVING

311 calories / 39 g carbohydrates / 4 g fiber / 5 g sugars / 12 g protein / 13 g total fat / 1.5 g saturated fat / 99 mg sodium

SPINACH BARLEY SALAD WITH GORGONZOLA AND TOASTED WALNUTS

Let's be honest: Gorgonzola packs a flavor punch that will have you scooping yourself another serving of salad. But thanks to that flavor, you don't need much to spice up your dish. Adding a grain, like barley, makes this salad a complete meal and a good source of complex carbohydrates.

MAKES 4 SERVINGS // TOTAL TIME: 20 MINUTES, PLUS 30 MINUTES CHILLING TIME

- 2 **cups quick-cooking pearl barley**
- 2 **tablespoons chopped walnuts**
- 3 **tablespoons sherry vinegar or red wine vinegar**
- ½ **teaspoon Dijon mustard**
- 2 **tablespoons extra-virgin olive oil**
- 1 **ounce Gorgonzola cheese, finely crumbled (about ¼ cup)**
- 6 **cups baby spinach, shredded**
- ¼ **cup sliced red onion**
  Salt and ground black pepper, to taste

Cook the barley according to the package directions.

Meanwhile, in a small dry skillet over medium heat, toast the walnuts for 8 minutes, or until fragrant and just beginning to take on color.

In a small bowl, whisk together the vinegar and mustard. Whisk in the oil until well blended, then whisk the cheese into the mixture.

In a serving bowl, combine the cooked barley, spinach, onion, walnuts, and salt and pepper to taste. Toss gently. Stir in the vinaigrette, then cover and refrigerate for at least 30 minutes to allow the flavors to blend.

NUTRITION PER SERVING   372 calories / 61 g carbohydrates / 10 g fiber / 1 g sugars / 11 g protein / 12 g total fat / 3 g saturated fat / 522 mg sodium

ASIAN HARMONY BEAN AND BROWN RICE SALAD

This "salad" is hardly your traditional lettuce-with-dressing dish. It's packed with veggies, rice, and beans for a hearty, protein-rich, filling, and colorful meal. Bring leftovers to work for a healthy lunch your coworkers will envy. Plan ahead and prepare an extra 2 cups brown basmati rice the next time you have it for dinner. Go with agave nectar instead of honey to make this dish vegan.

MAKES 8 SERVINGS // TOTAL TIME: 20 MINUTES

¼ cup fresh orange juice

¼ cup prepared green tea, cooled

¼ cup rice vinegar

2 tablespoons honey or agave nectar

1 teaspoon grated fresh ginger

1 teaspoon minced garlic

1 teaspoon ground coriander

1½ teaspoons toasted sesame oil

¼ teaspoon salt

¼ teaspoon ground black pepper

½ cup olive oil

1 can (15 ounces) black beans, rinsed and drained

2 cups shelled edamame, cooked

2 cups cooked and cooled brown basmati rice

1 can (8 ounces) sliced water chestnuts, drained and chopped

½ cup chopped celery

½ cup chopped red bell pepper

½ cup slivered almonds

¼ cup chopped fresh cilantro

In a large bowl, whisk together the orange juice, tea, vinegar, honey or agave, ginger, garlic, coriander, sesame oil, salt, and black pepper. Whisk in the oil until emulsified. Stir in the black beans, edamame, rice, water chestnuts, celery, bell pepper, almonds, and cilantro, tossing to coat well.

NUTRITION PER SERVING 326 calories / 29 g carbohydrates / 6 g fiber / 7 g sugars / 9 g protein / 20 g total fat / 2.5 g saturated fat / 220 mg sodium

8

SAUCES & SPREADS

SPICY MANGO BBQ SAUCE

This isn't your average BBQ sauce, thanks to a kick from Asian chili sauce and refreshing chunks of mango. Top your favorite veggie burger, or for something completely different, spread over a freshly grilled ear of corn. To make this sauce vegan, use agave nectar instead of honey.

MAKES 3 CUPS // TOTAL TIME: 40 MINUTES

1	cup mango chutney, finely chopped if the pieces are large
1	cup ketchup
¾	cup honey or agave nectar
½	cup apple juice or apple cider
½	cup dark rum
¼	cup apple cider vinegar
1	piece (3") fresh ginger, peeled and grated
5	cloves garlic, minced
3	tablespoons tomato paste
2	tablespoons vegan Worcestershire sauce
2	tablespoons Dijon mustard
1	tablespoon Asian chili-garlic sauce
1	tablespoon soy sauce
¼	teaspoon ground black pepper

In a large saucepan, whisk together the chutney, ketchup, honey or agave, apple juice or cider, rum, vinegar, ginger, garlic, tomato paste, Worcestershire sauce, mustard, chili-garlic sauce, soy sauce, and pepper. Bring to a boil over medium heat, stirring constantly. Reduce the heat to low and simmer, stirring occasionally, for 30 minutes, or until the sauce is thickened and slightly reduced.

NUTRITION PER SERVING (1 TABLESPOON)

51 calories / 11 g carbohydrates / 0 g fiber / 9 g sugars / 0 g protein / 0 g total fat / 0 g saturated fat / 158 mg sodium

CREAMY VEGGIE DIP

Choose high-oleic safflower oil for the highest monounsaturated fatty acid (MUFA) content. You'll get more bang for your healthy-fat buck (75 percent versus 12 percent in olive oil). Cutting the recipe with cottage cheese reduces the amount of sour cream needed, making this a better-for-you-but-still-creamy dip.

MAKES 8 SERVINGS // TOTAL TIME: 10 MINUTES, PLUS 1 HOUR CHILLING TIME

⅓   cup reduced-fat sour cream

2   tablespoons safflower or olive oil

1   cup 1% small-curd cottage cheese

¼   cup finely chopped red onion

1   jalapeño chile pepper, seeded and finely chopped

1   large clove garlic, minced

1   tablespoon fresh lemon juice

½   teaspoon vegan Worcestershire sauce

¼   teaspoon salt

In a large bowl, whisk together the sour cream and oil until smooth and creamy. Stir in the cottage cheese, onion, jalapeño pepper, garlic, lemon juice, Worcestershire sauce, and salt. Cover and chill for at least 1 hour before serving.

NUTRITION PER SERVING (3 TABLESPOONS) 70 calories / 2 g carbohydrates / 0 g fiber / 2 g sugars / 4 g protein / 5 g total fat / 1 g saturated fat / 198 mg sodium

SAUCES & SPREADS

AUTUMN PEAR SALSA

Dip your favorite tortilla chip in this fruit- and antioxidant-packed salsa for a refreshing, feel-good snack. Thanks to the grapefruit, this salsa will also help hydrate you after a sweaty run.

MAKES 4 CUPS // TOTAL TIME: 10 MINUTES, PLUS 1 HOUR CHILLING TIME

1 **large pink grapefruit**

2 **pears, peeled, cored, and diced**

½ **cup dried tart cherries**

2 **tablespoons minced red onion**

½ **teaspoon grated lime zest**

2 **tablespoons fresh lime juice**

1 **clove garlic, minced**

¼ **fresh jalapeño chile pepper, minced**

Using a paring knife, peel the grapefruit, cutting off all the white pith and membrane. Cut down either side of the membranes to separate the fruit segments, and release the sections into a large bowl. Cut the sections into ½" chunks. Add the pears, cherries, onion, lime zest, lime juice, garlic, and jalapeño pepper. Refrigerate for at least 1 hour.

NUTRITION PER SERVING (¼ CUP)

34 calories / 9 g carbohydrates / 2 g fiber / 5 g sugars / 0 g protein / 0 g total fat / 0 g saturated fat / 0 mg sodium

ROASTED VEGGIE DIP

Whether you're trying to sneak veggies into your kids' diets or your own, this dip is a great way to do it. Become a veggie superstar by using crudités with this dip—but we won't tell if you prefer baked pita crisps.

MAKES 3 CUPS // TOTAL TIME: 40 MINUTES

- 1 **medium yellow squash, cut into large chunks**
- 1 **medium zucchini, cut into large chunks**
- 1 **cucumber, halved, seeded, and cut into large chunks**
- 1 **bell pepper, any color, cut into large chunks**
- 1 **red onion, cut into large chunks**
- 2 **cloves garlic, minced**
- ¼ **teaspoon salt**
- ¼ **teaspoon ground black pepper or chili powder**
- 1 **tablespoon tomato paste**

Preheat the oven to 400°F. Coat a baking sheet with cooking spray.

Place the squash, zucchini, cucumber, bell pepper, and onion on the baking sheet and coat with cooking spray. Sprinkle with the garlic, salt, and black pepper or chili powder. Bake, turning once, for 30 minutes, or until the vegetables are tender and lightly browned.

Transfer the vegetables to a blender or food processor. Add the tomato paste and puree until just blended, but with some texture. Transfer to a serving bowl and serve warm or cold.

PRO TIP

This dip can be frozen, so you can make it ahead and then serve as a crowd-pleasing appetizer.

NUTRITION PER SERVING (2 TABLESPOONS)

8 calories / 2 g carbohydrates / 0 g fiber / 1 g sugars / 0 g protein / 0 g total fat / 0 g saturated fat / 33 mg sodium

WALNUT PÂTÉ

This richly flavored, brain-healthy vegetarian pâté is the perfect stand-in for a traditional pâté. Walnuts are one of the best foods for your mind and may even reduce the risk of Alzheimer's disease. For best results, serve at room temperature.

MAKES 1 CUP // TOTAL TIME: 30 MINUTES

- 1 tablespoon canola oil
- 1 cup walnuts
- ¼ onion, chopped
- 2 tablespoons raisins
- ½ teaspoon dried thyme
- ¼ teaspoon paprika
- 1 tablespoon roasted garlic (from a jar)
- 2 tablespoons fresh lemon juice
- 2 tablespoons chopped fresh parsley
- ⅛ teaspoon salt
  Ground black pepper, to taste

In a medium skillet over medium heat, heat the oil until sizzling. Add the walnuts. Cook, stirring occasionally, for 3 minutes, or until toasted. Add the onion, raisins, thyme, and paprika. Cook, stirring, for 5 minutes, or until the onion is softened. Add the garlic. Stir just until the garlic is incorporated. Remove from the heat. Cool to room temperature.

Transfer the mixture to a food processor or blender. Process or blend, scraping the bowl as needed, for 3 minutes, or until a coarse paste forms. Add the lemon juice, parsley, salt, and pepper to taste. Pulse just until combined. Serve immediately or refrigerate for up to 1 week.

NUTRITION PER SERVING (2 TABLESPOONS)

113 calories / 5 g carbohydrates / 1 g fiber / 2 g sugars / 2 g protein / 10 g total fat / 1 g saturated fat / 38 mg sodium

APRICOT CHUTNEY

Chutney is often used to top meat, but it also serves as a great, low-calorie flavor booster in oatmeal and yogurt, and on toast or pancakes. Adding cayenne pepper is a calorie-free way to spice up any dish without extra salt or fat. To make this a vegan chutney, use agave instead of honey.

MAKES 3 CUPS // TOTAL TIME: 35 MINUTES

- **2 cups dried apricots**
- **3 to 4 cups boiling water**
- **3 tablespoons honey or agave nectar**
- **1½ tablespoons apple cider vinegar**
- **1 teaspoon minced fresh ginger, or ½ teaspoon ground ginger**
- **½ teaspoon ground coriander**
- **Pinch of cayenne pepper**
- **½ cup raw cashews, coarsely chopped**
- **½ cup raisins**

In a heatproof medium bowl, combine the apricots and enough boiling water to cover. Let sit for 30 minutes, or until soft. Drain and chop the apricots. Return to the bowl. Add the honey or agave, vinegar, ginger, coriander, and cayenne and mix well. Add the cashews and raisins and mix well again. Store in the refrigerator for up to 2 weeks.

NUTRITION PER SERVING (2 TABLESPOONS)

56 calories / 12 g carbohydrates / 1 g fiber / 10 g sugars / 1 g protein / 1 g total fat / 0 g saturated fat / 2 mg sodium

BOURBON MUSTARD SAUCE

Serve this tangy, spicy sauce over grilled veggie kebabs or atop a veggie burger. Mustard is a great vehicle for flavor, without the fat and calories that come with traditional mayonnaise. And it's vegan!

MAKES 2 CUPS // TOTAL TIME: 40 MINUTES

1¼ cups light molasses
1   cup Dijon mustard
¼   cup bourbon
1   tablespoon vegan Worcestershire sauce
2   tablespoons dry mustard
2   tablespoons mustard seeds
½   teaspoon kosher salt
¼   teaspoon ground allspice

In a medium saucepan, whisk together the molasses, mustard, bourbon, Worcestershire sauce, dry mustard, mustard seeds, salt, and allspice. Bring to a simmer and cook, stirring occasionally, for 20 to 30 minutes, or until the sauce begins to thicken. Cool to room temperature before serving, as it will thicken as it cools. Store in the refrigerator for up to 2 weeks.

NUTRITION PER SERVING (1 TABLESPOON)

47 calories / 10 g carbohydrates / 0 g fiber / 9 g sugars / 0 g protein / 0 g total fat / 0 g saturated fat / 139 mg sodium

CILANTRO-PEAR VINAIGRETTE

Using fresh herbs to season dishes, spreads, or dressings is an almost calorie- and sodium-free way to add flavor. Cilantro has a powerful flavor to spice up any dressing, and it's high in antioxidants. And pear makes this dressing perfectly refreshing for a hot summer day.

MAKES 2 CUPS // TOTAL TIME: 5 MINUTES

½   **cup fresh cilantro leaves**

1   **small pear, cored and quartered**

1   **clove garlic, peeled**
    Juice of 1 lemon

2   **tablespoons white wine vinegar**

½   **cup extra-virgin olive oil**

In a blender, combine the cilantro, pear, garlic, lemon juice, and vinegar. Blend until smooth. On low speed, drizzle in the oil and blend to emulsify. Serve immediately or store, covered, in the refrigerator for up to 4 days. Shake to redistribute if settling occurs.

NUTRITION PER SERVING (2 TABLESPOONS)

69 calories / 2 g carbohydrates / 0 g fiber / 1 g sugars / 0 g protein / 7 g total fat / 1 g saturated fat / 0 mg sodium

CREAMY GREEN DIP

Avocado packs a nutritious punch in this creamy dip, thanks to its healthy fat, fiber, and vitamin C. Serve with your favorite whole grain crackers and fresh veggies.

MAKES 1 CUP // TOTAL TIME: 5 MINUTES

2	**tablespoons mayonnaise**
¼	**cup rice vinegar**
1	**clove garlic**
½	**avocado, pitted and peeled**
½	**cup fresh dill**
½	**cup fresh mint**
½	**cup fresh cilantro**
½	**cup scallions, green part only**
¼	**cup olive oil**
½	**cup water**
½	**teaspoon fine sea salt**

In a blender or food processor, combine the mayonnaise, vinegar, garlic, avocado, dill, mint, cilantro, scallions, oil, water, and salt. Blend or process until smooth. Store, covered, in the refrigerator for up to 4 days.

NUTRITION PER SERVING (¼ CUP)

215 calories / 4 g carbohydrates / 2 g fiber / 1 g sugars / 1 g protein / 22 g total fat / 3 g saturated fat / 292 mg sodium

LIME-SESAME DRESSING

Lime juice is brimming with vitamin C, which studies show may help runners avoid the common cold. Drizzle this dressing over your favorite salad for an instant Asian twist. Choose agave instead of honey for a vegan-friendly dressing.

MAKES ½ CUP // TOTAL TIME: 5 MINUTES

Juice of 1 lime

2 tablespoons light sesame oil

1 tablespoon soy sauce

2 teaspoons Asian chili sauce, like sriracha or sambal oelek

2 teaspoons honey or agave nectar

In a bowl, whisk together the lime juice, oil, soy sauce, chili sauce, and honey or agave. Store, covered, in the refrigerator for up to 1 week.

NUTRITION PER SERVING (2 TABLESPOONS)

81 calories / 5 g carbohydrates / 0 g fiber / 4 g sugars / 1 g protein / 7 g total fat / 1 g saturated fat / 250 mg sodium

SWEET AND SALTY PISTACHIO BUTTER

Change up your traditional nut butter with pistachios, a good source of copper for immune health. Pistachios are also high in the B vitamin thiamin, which helps your body turn carbs into fuel for running. This spread is great with goat cheese, pretzels, or multigrain crackers.

MAKES ½ CUP // TOTAL TIME: 5 MINUTES

1 **cup salted roasted pistachios**

2 **tablespoons canola oil**

1 **tablespoon honey**

In a food processor, combine the pistachios and oil. Process for 4 minutes, stopping to scrape down the bowl as needed. Scrape the nut butter into a bowl and stir in the honey. Store in an airtight container in the refrigerator for up to 1 week.

NUTRITION PER SERVING (2 TABLESPOONS)

250 calories / 13 g carbohydrates / 3 g fiber / 7 g sugars / 6 g protein / 21 g total fat / 2.5 g saturated fat / 132 mg sodium

9 DESSERT

FIGS WITH RICOTTA AND WILDFLOWER HONEY

Eat like an elite! Ancient Greek athletes (like Pheidippides, who ran from Marathon to Athens to declare the Greeks had won the Battle of Marathon) lived on fresh figs. High in fiber, they are a seasonal treat and pair perfectly with honey and ricotta cheese.

MAKES 6 SERVINGS // TOTAL TIME: 10 MINUTES

12 **large fresh figs**

¾ **cup whole-milk ricotta cheese, at room temperature**

6 **tablespoons wildflower honey**

Quarter the figs and arrange on plates. Add 1 or 2 spoonfuls of ricotta and a generous drizzle of honey to each plate.

NUTRITION PER SERVING

213 calories / 43 g carbohydrates / 4 g fiber / 38 g sugars / 5 g protein / 4 g total fat / 2.5 g saturated fat / 28 mg sodium

APPLE-MAPLE COFFEE CAKE

This cake is what fall is all about: spices and apples that pair perfectly with a cup of warm apple cider or coffee. Serve as dessert or with coffee after a long run in the crisp autumn air. You can also make this with pears and golden raisins instead of apples and currants for something different.

MAKES 12 SERVINGS // TOTAL TIME: 45 MINUTES

2	cups + 3 tablespoons whole wheat pastry flour
1	teaspoon baking soda
½	teaspoon salt
¾	cup (1½ sticks) unsalted butter, divided
¾	cup buttermilk
1	egg
½	cup maple syrup
2	apples, cored, peeled, and sliced
2	tablespoons dried currants
½	cup coarsely chopped walnuts
½	cup maple sugar
½	teaspoon ground cinnamon
¼	teaspoon ground cloves
¼	teaspoon ground nutmeg

Preheat the oven to 375°F. Butter a 9" round baking pan.

In a large bowl, whisk together the flour, baking soda, and salt. Cube ½ cup (1 stick) of the butter. With your fingers or a pastry blender, cut in the cubed butter until the mixture resembles coarse crumbs.

In a small bowl, combine the buttermilk, egg, and maple syrup. Pour into the flour mixture and beat just until smooth. Pour the batter into the baking pan. Arrange the apple slices on top. Sprinkle the currants and nuts evenly over the apples.

In a small saucepan, melt the remaining ¼ cup (½ stick) butter.

In a small bowl, combine the maple sugar, cinnamon, cloves, and nutmeg. Sprinkle the sugar mixture over the fruit and nuts and drizzle with the melted butter.

Bake for 25 minutes, or until a toothpick inserted into the center of the cake comes out clean. Let cool slightly before cutting and serving.

NUTRITION PER SERVING

299 calories / 37 g carbohydrates / 4 g fiber / 18 g sugars / 4 g protein / 16 g total fat / 8 g saturated fat / 228 mg sodium

RED VELVET BROWNIES

Want to know a secret? Red velvet is really just food coloring. Ditch the artificial additives and use beets instead. They'll not only add color, but also add moisture and sweetness that don't overpower the chocolate flavor. Plus, the nitrates found in beets may boost performance thanks to their ability to increase oxygen flow to your muscles (although you'd need to eat way more beets than in these brownies to reap that benefit!). Sneaking in some quinoa makes this a healthier treat thanks to its fiber and plant protein.

MAKES 12 SERVINGS // TOTAL TIME: 55 MINUTES

½ **pound beets, chopped**
¾ **cup hot coffee**
6 **ounces unsweetened baking chocolate, chopped**
⅓ **cup unsweetened cocoa powder**
¼ **cup coconut oil**
2 **eggs**
¾ **cup sugar**
2 **teaspoons vanilla extract**
¾ **cup quinoa flour**
1 **teaspoon ground cinnamon**
1 **teaspoon ground ginger**
½ **teaspoon baking powder**
¼ **teaspoon salt**
½ **cup chopped walnuts**

Preheat the oven to 350°F. Grease an 8" × 8" baking pan.

Steam the beets for 15 minutes, or until tender. Transfer to a food processor and finely chop.

In a large bowl, whisk together the hot coffee, chocolate, cocoa powder, and oil. Let sit for 5 minutes, then stir until smooth. Stir in the beets, eggs, sugar, and vanilla.

In a medium bowl, mix the quinoa flour, cinnamon, ginger, baking powder, and salt. Add to the wet ingredients. Stir gently until combined. Fold in the nuts. Pour the mixture into the baking pan. Bake for 20 minutes, or until a toothpick inserted into the center comes out with a few moist crumbs attached.

NUTRITION PER SERVING 250 calories / 26 g carbohydrates / 5 g fiber / 14 g sugars / 5 g protein / 17 g total fat / 9 g saturated fat / 102 mg sodium

TEFF-CHOCOLATE PUDDING

If you can't run like the Ethiopians, you can *at least* eat like them. The secret ingredient in this chocolaty pudding is teff, a whole grain staple in the running phenoms' diets. As it cooks, teff releases starches, creating a thick, smooth consistency—perfect for pudding.

MAKES 4 SERVINGS // TOTAL TIME: 30 MINUTES, PLUS 2 HOURS CHILLING TIME

THE RUNNER'S WORLD VEGETARIAN COOKBOOK

2   cups water
½   cup teff grain (not flour)
4   teaspoons chopped hazelnuts
4   teaspoons unsweetened flaked coconut
1   banana
⅓   cup well-stirred full-fat coconut milk
3   tablespoons molasses
3   tablespoons unsweetened cocoa powder
2   teaspoons vanilla extract
½   teaspoon ground ginger
¼   teaspoon ground cloves
     Pinch of salt

In a medium saucepan, bring the water and teff to a boil. Reduce the heat and simmer for 15 minutes, or until the water is absorbed.

Meanwhile, in a dry skillet over medium heat, toast the hazelnuts for 6 to 8 minutes, or until lightly golden and fragrant. Remove from the skillet and repeat with the flaked coconut, toasting it for 4 to 5 minutes.

Transfer the teff to a blender along with the banana, coconut milk, molasses, cocoa powder, vanilla, ginger, cloves, and salt. Blend until smooth. Transfer to a bowl and chill for 2 hours. Top each serving with the toasted hazelnuts and flaked coconut.

NUTRITION PER SERVING

232 calories / 39 g carbohydrates / 6 g fiber / 15 g sugars / 5 g protein / 8 g total fat / 5 g saturated fat / 59 mg sodium

FLAX BANANA BREAD

There's nothing like creamy banana bread. Except when you add flaxseed, a source of fiber and good-for-you fat. Add a half cup of dark chocolate chips to satisfy your chocolate craving, or top with a scoop of vanilla ice cream.

MAKES 10 SERVINGS // TOTAL TIME: 1 HOUR 10 MINUTES

- ½ **cup packed light brown sugar**
- ½ **cup buttermilk**
- 1 **egg or flax egg (3 tablespoons water and 1 tablespoon ground flaxseed)**
- 3 **tablespoons canola oil**
- ¾ **cup all-purpose flour**
- ½ **cup whole wheat flour**
- ¾ **cup ground flaxseed**
- 1 **teaspoon baking powder**
- 1 **teaspoon baking soda**
- ⅛ **teaspoon salt**
- 1 **cup mashed very ripe bananas**

Preheat the oven to 350°F. Coat a nonstick 8" × 4" loaf pan with cooking spray.

In a large bowl, combine the brown sugar, buttermilk, egg, and oil. Whisk until smooth.

In a medium bowl, whisk together the all-purpose flour, whole wheat flour, flaxseed, baking powder, baking soda, and salt. Add to the wet ingredients and stir just until blended; do not overmix. Add the bananas and stir to mix. Pour into the loaf pan.

Bake for 40 to 50 minutes, or until a knife inserted into the center comes out clean. Remove the pan to a wire rack and cool for 10 minutes. Turn the bread out of the pan and cool completely. Cut into 10 slices.

PRO TIP

For best results, choose very ripe bananas, place them in a blender or food processor, and puree until smooth.

NUTRITION PER SERVING

213 calories / 30 g carbohydrates / 3 g fiber / 14 g sugars / 5 g protein / 9 g total fat / 0.5 g saturated fat / 219 mg sodium

STEEL-CUT OATMEAL RAISIN COOKIES

Steel-cut oats can improve heart health and keep you feeling full, so you won't eat the whole tray of cookies. Mixed with raisins and walnuts, these cookies could easily be a breakfast—we won't tell.

MAKES 24 SERVINGS // TOTAL TIME: 1 HOUR 30 MINUTES

- 1⅓ cups cooked steel-cut oats
- ¾ cup whole wheat flour
- 1½ teaspoons ground cinnamon
- ¾ teaspoon baking powder
- ¼ cup + 2 tablespoons coconut oil
- ¼ cup + 1 tablespoon packed brown sugar
- 1 flax egg (3 tablespoons water and 1 tablespoon ground flaxseed)
- 2 teaspoons vanilla extract
- ½ cup chopped walnuts
- ½ cup raisins, lightly chopped

Preheat the oven to 300°F.

Spread the cooked oats onto a baking sheet rubbed with coconut oil and bake for 30 minutes, or until they begin to dry out, stirring every 10 minutes. Cool completely.

Increase the oven temperature to 375°F.

In a medium bowl, stir together the flour, cinnamon, baking powder, and cooled oats.

In a large bowl, beat together the oil and brown sugar until combined and lightened in color. Add the flax egg and vanilla and beat to combine completely. Stir the flour mixture into the sugar mixture until incorporated. Stir in the walnuts and raisins.

Drop the dough by heaping tablespoons onto an ungreased baking sheet and flatten slightly. Bake for 15 to 20 minutes, or until golden brown. Refrigerate leftovers.

NUTRITION PER COOKIE

97 calories / 12 g carbohydrates / 1 g fiber / 5 g sugars / 2 g protein / 6 g total fat / 3 g saturated fat / 17 mg sodium

BANANA CHOCOLATE TACOS

Tacos aren't just for dinner. This sweet combo is a good source of potassium, which promotes muscle function, thanks to the bananas. And dark chocolate is high in disease-fighting antioxidants.

MAKES 4 SERVINGS // TOTAL TIME: 15 MINUTES

- 1 cup part-skim ricotta cheese
- 2 tablespoons almond butter
- 1 tablespoon maple syrup
- 1 teaspoon orange zest
- 1 teaspoon vanilla extract
- 2 ounces dark chocolate, chopped
- ½ teaspoon ground cinnamon
- 4 whole wheat tortillas (6" diameter)
- 4 small bananas, sliced into ½" pieces
- ¼ cup unsweetened flaked coconut, toasted (optional)

In a small bowl, mix together the ricotta, almond butter, maple syrup, orange zest, and vanilla.

In a separate small microwaveable bowl, microwave the chocolate on high power in 20-second intervals, stirring between each interval, until melted. Stir in the cinnamon.

Heat the tortillas according to the package directions. Spread the ricotta mixture on the tortillas and top with the banana slices. Drizzle the chocolate sauce over the top. Sprinkle on the flaked coconut, if desired.

PRO TIP

Save a taco for breakfast—this combo is similar to a sweet crepe!

NUTRITION PER SERVING   439 calories / 53 g carbohydrates / 13 g fiber / 23 g sugars / 14 g protein / 20 g total fat / 9.5 g saturated fat / 342 mg sodium

CHOCOLATE TOFU PIE

Full disclosure: This is the reason I married my husband—it's his mom's recipe. Don't be turned off by the combination of chocolate and tofu in this recipe. The latter is the vehicle for the former, and tofu means you're getting protein in your oh-so-rich and creamy dessert. The brand specified, Mori-Nu, will make your pie nice and firm. Other brands of silken tofu taste just as good but are much softer.

MAKES 12 SERVINGS // TOTAL TIME: 45 MINUTES, PLUS 1 HOUR CHILLING TIME

14 graham crackers (8 ounces)

4   ounces unsalted butter or coconut oil, melted

14 ounces bittersweet chocolate, chopped

2   packages (about 12 ounces each) firm silken tofu (such as Mori-Nu), drained

½   cup maple syrup
    Pinch of kosher salt

Preheat the oven to 350°F. Crush the graham crackers with a rolling pin or grind in a food processor until fine and uniform.

Pour the cracker crumbs into a 9" deep-dish pie plate. Add the melted butter or oil. Using a fork, mix the butter or oil into the crumbs until the mixture resembles wet sand. Press the mixture firmly and evenly into the bottom and up the sides of the pie plate. Bake for 10 minutes, or until fragrant and golden. Remove from the oven and let cool completely.

In a double boiler (see page 255 for instructions) or in a microwave, melt the chocolate until smooth. In a food processor, process the tofu until smooth. Add the warm melted chocolate and pulse until completely combined and smooth. Add the maple syrup and salt.

Pour the chocolate filling into the cooled pie crust. Chill for 1 hour, or until firm. Slice and serve.

PRO TIP

Choose coconut oil instead of butter to make this decadent dessert vegan-friendly.

NUTRITION PER SERVING — 378 calories / 42 g carbohydrates / 3 g fiber / 29 g sugars / 5 g protein / 21 g total fat / 11.5 g saturated fat / 109 mg sodium

CHOCOLATE AVOCADO MOUSSE

For a decadent, guilt-free mousse, avocado is the secret. High in healthy fat, it serves as a creamy base for this chocolate treat. Eat as is or spread over your favorite cookies, waffles, or pancakes.

MAKES 4 SERVINGS // TOTAL TIME: 30 MINUTES, PLUS 1 HOUR CHILLING TIME

4   ounces dark chocolate, chopped

2   ripe avocados, pitted and peeled

¼   to ⅓ cup canned unsweetened coconut milk

¼   cup unsweetened cocoa powder

1   teaspoon vanilla extract

⅓   cup maple syrup

    Pinch of sea salt

    Whipped cream or coconut cream (optional)

In a double boiler (see page 255 for instructions) or in a microwave, melt the chocolate until smooth. Let cool.

In a food processor, combine the cooled chocolate with the avocados, ¼ cup coconut milk, adding more if the mixture is too thick, cocoa powder, vanilla, maple syrup, and salt. Process until smooth and creamy. Spoon into 4 ramekins or dessert dishes and chill for at least 1 hour.

Serve with a dollop of whipped cream (or whipped coconut cream to keep this treat vegan), if desired.

DESSERT

NUTRITION PER SERVING 429 calories / 47 g carbohydrates / 11 g fiber / 32 g sugars / 5 g protein / 28 g total fat / 10.5 g saturated fat / 44 mg sodium

DARK CHOCOLATE ALMOND BUTTER DATE TRUFFLES WITH SEA SALT

Over the years this recipe has been modified from the original recipe created by Leah Rosenfeld, a friend of Matt Llano's, to yield the most refined finished product. This healthy dessert is sweet and very easy to make—you need only four ingredients! Almond butter is a great source of healthy fat and plant protein, and dates are good sources of vitamin B6, magnesium, and potassium.

MAKES 36 TRUFFLES // TOTAL TIME: 30 MINUTES, PLUS 30 MINUTES CHILLING TIME

20 to 24 dates, pitted

2 to 4 tablespoons almond butter (or your favorite nut butter)

¾ to 1 cup dark chocolate chips (60% cacao)

Coarse sea salt

Line a baking sheet with parchment paper.

In a food processor, combine the dates and nut butter. Process until a large ball forms, scraping down the sides of the bowl if the mixture sticks. Scoop 1 heaping teaspoon of the date mixture and roll into a 1" ball. Place the rolled date ball on the baking sheet, and continue with the remaining mixture.

Place the chocolate chips in a medium heatproof bowl. Bring 1" of water to a simmer in a saucepan. Set the bowl over the saucepan (make sure the water doesn't touch the bottom of the bowl) and stir for 3 to 5 minutes, or until the chocolate is melted and smooth.

Roll the date balls in the melted chocolate to coat evenly. Using a fork, lift the date balls out of the chocolate, allowing any excess chocolate to drip back into the bowl. Return the date balls to the baking sheet and sprinkle with coarse sea salt. Refrigerate for at least 30 minutes, or until the chocolate has set.

NUTRITION PER SERVING (1 TRUFFLE)

40 calories / 6 g carbohydrates / 1 g fiber / 5 g sugars / 1 g protein / 2 g total fat / 1 g saturated fat / 87 mg sodium

RAW CARDAMOM-SPICED FRUIT CRISP

This summer dessert is sweet, thanks to the natural sugar in fruit and maple syrup, which means it's also teeming with fiber and antioxidants. Serve leftovers atop yogurt (regular or dairy-free) for a breakfast treat.

MAKES 2 SERVINGS // TOTAL TIME: 15 MINUTES

- 2 peaches, pitted and chopped
- 1 cup blackberries
- 1 tablespoon maple syrup
- 6 dates, pitted and coarsely chopped
- ¼ cup walnuts, coarsely chopped
- ¼ cup pistachios, coarsely chopped
- ¼ cup old-fashioned rolled oats
- ¼ teaspoon ground cardamom
- ⅛ teaspoon ground cloves

In a bowl, combine the peaches and blackberries and toss with the maple syrup.

In a small bowl, combine the dates, walnuts, pistachios, oats, cardamom, and cloves.

Sprinkle the nut crumble over the top of the fruit and store in the refrigerator until you're ready to eat.

NUTRITION PER SERVING

397 calories / 57 g carbohydrates / 11 g fiber / 37 g sugars / 10 g protein / 18 g total fat / 2 g saturated fat / 8 mg sodium

ACKNOWLEDGMENTS

▶ The acknowledgments page of a book, as it's become clear to me, is basically an award acceptance speech you don't have to memorize. Which is good, because there are so many people to thank that in an actual speech I'd certainly forget someone.

First and foremost, I need to thank my husband, Jeff. His recipes appear on these pages because he's a guy who can do it all. If it weren't for his support, I never would have made the move to Pennsylvania to take my dream job at *Runner's World* (okay, maybe I would have, but I would have missed him very much), and I never would have had the opportunity to write and edit this cookbook. He also retrieved this manuscript from the bowels of my computer when I thought all hope was lost *and* figured out why my spell checker wasn't working (the language was somehow set to Russian). I love you, and I'm sorry for being such a picky eater.

Thank you to Tish Hamilton, who took a chance on me when she hired me at *Runner's World,* and who has taught me more than she'll ever realize about writing, editing, running, and life. To my #RunSquad: Meghan Kita, Ali Nolan, and Hannah McGoldrick: proof that your coworkers can become some of your best friends. And a bonus when they'll run and eat with you.

Jen Keiser in the Rodale library did some of the most nitty-gritty, thankless work for this book. She made my life so much easier, and for that, there are no words.

Thanks to Mark Weinstein, who approached me for this project when I was just a few months into my job as food and nutrition editor. You gave me such a cool opportunity, and I'll be forever grateful. Especially when the royalty checks start coming in. Thank you to the team at Crown Publishing who shepherded this book to production. Thank you to Trisha de Guzman, who read every word of this manuscript and didn't go too hard on me.

Pam Nisevich Bede is a woman who really can do it all: She works full-time, has a private dietitian practice, has three young kids, runs really fast, and is a regular columnist for RunnersWorld.com. She is also the RD expert who reviewed every recipe with a fine-tooth comb.

This book would not have been possible in its pristine, final form without the Rodale Test Kitchen. Juli Roberts, Jen Kushnier, and Amy Fritch are heroes among us. They vetted and edited every single recipe, and, at least to my face, didn't complain once. They also fed me. A lot.

Thanks to my parents and siblings, who have always supported my work and aren't afraid to show how proud they are. I love you. And finally, thanks to my kiddo, Finn, whose imminent arrival pushed me to submit my manuscript early.

(Okay, two more: This book was written with much company from our cats, The Great Catsby and The Wizard of Paws. If there's a random typo remaining, I blame them. They love to walk on the keyboard.)

THE RUNNER'S PANTRY

Life is busy. Fitting in a run may relieve stress, but it doesn't give you more time to prepare healthy, nutritious meals. Keep your pantry, fridge, and freezer stocked with these staples so you can quickly throw together a meal without sacrificing your workout (or your sanity).

Canned Beans and Dried Lentils

Chickpeas
White beans (such as cannellini and great northern)
Dark and light kidney beans
Pinto beans
Black beans
Red, brown, and green dried lentils

Grains

Brown rice
Bulgur
Barley
Quinoa
Oats (old-fashioned and steel-cut)
Whole wheat pastry flour

Pasta and Noodles

Whole wheat pasta
White (semolina) pasta
Soba noodles

Long-Lasting Produce

Potatoes (sweet, baking, Yukon Gold, or red-skinned)
Onions
Garlic
Carrots
Celery
Canned tomatoes (whole and diced)
Frozen fruits and vegetables

Dried Fruits

Dried tart cherries
Raisins
Dried blueberries
Dried apricots

Nuts and Seeds

Walnuts
Almonds
Pecans
Nut butters
Ground flaxseed

Oils and Vinegars

Extra-virgin olive oil
Canola oil
Walnut or flaxseed oil
Balsamic vinegar
Rice vinegar or sherry vinegar

Flavorings

Dried herbs and spices
Jarred pesto
Roasted red peppers
Sun-dried tomatoes
Bottled stir-fry sauce
Soy sauce
Dijon mustard
Vegetable broth

RECIPE CONTRIBUTORS

We thank these food writers, recipe developers, chefs, dietitians, and elite runners, whose recipes appear in this book.

ANNE ALEXANDER
Pumpkin Pie Trail Mix
    Popcorn

JAN BELL
Roasted Veggie Dip

DAVID BONOM
Watercress and Radicchio
    Salad with Mustard
    Vinaigrette

JENNIFER BRIGHT REICH
Iced Spiced Cocoa Latte

CHRISTINA CAIRA
Fennel Cauliflower
    Chowder

MAUREEN CALLAHAN
Spinach Barley Salad with
    Gorgonzola and Toasted
    Walnuts

AMY CANTOR
Walnut Sweet Potato Bread
Roasted Chickpeas with
    Cabbage Slaw
Peanut Butter Sweet
    Potato Soup

SOLMAZ CHANDLER
Quinoa Breakfast Porridge
Carrot Hummus
Butternut Squash Soup
Heirloom Tomato
    Gazpacho
Black Bean and Sweet
    Potato Chili

STEPHANIE CLARKE
Ginger-Spiked Peach Fizz
Cardamom-Ginger Chai Tea

Chili-Lime Kale Chips
Cilantro-Pear Vinaigrette
Creamy Green Dip
Steel-Cut Oatmeal Raisin
    Cookies

ANNE EGAN
Spring Risotto
Asian Harmony Bean and
    Brown Rice Salad
Walnut Pâté

DAVID FEDER
Watercress and Radicchio
    Salad with Mustard
    Vinaigrette

SHALANE FLANAGAN
Coconut Curry Lentil Soup
Kale Farro Salad with
    Lemon-Miso Dressing

AMY FRITCH
"Eggy" Tofu Scramble

SANDRA GLUCK
Granola with Toasted
    Almonds and Cherries
Buckwheat Pancakes
Spinach and Feta Frittata
Mexican Coffee
Hot Gingered Cider with
    Lady Apples
Spinach-Tofu Puffs
Maple Pepitas
Flax and Oat Crackers
Tropical Fruit Bars
Double-Baked Sweet
    Potato Skins
Soba Pancake with
    Scallions and Ginger
Ratatouille
Herbed Coleslaw

Vegan "Creamed" Spinach
Israeli Couscous with Lime
    and Mint
Double Portobello Burgers
Roasted Root Vegetable
    Salad with Lemon-Dijon
    Vinaigrette
Spicy Mango BBQ Sauce
Autumn Pear Salsa
Apricot Chutney
Bourbon Mustard Sauce
Figs with Ricotta and
    Wildflower Honey
Apple-Maple Coffee Cake

AMY GORIN
Pumpkin Ricotta Waffles
Egg with Grits and
    Mushrooms
Espresso Almond Smoothie

MARGEAUX GRAY
Curry-Spiced Veggie
    Burgers

MONICA GULLON
Veggie Rolls with Mango-
    Ginger Dipping Sauce

TRACY HARRIS
Caprese Farro Salad

GAIL HAYES
5-Minute Coleslaw

MINDY HERMANN
Roasted Tomatoes Stuffed
    with Quinoa and Herbs
Cuban Rice and Beans

ANITA HIRSCH
Sweet Potato–Coconut
    Fritters

HEATHER MAYER IRVINE
Zucchini Bread
Avocado Toast
Baked Egg in Avocado
Greek Yogurt Bowl
Bee Pollen Popcorn
Banana Frozen "Yogurt"
Sesame Bok Choy
Butternut Squash Quinoa
    Bowl
Spicy Thai Noodles
Coconut Milk Rice
Veggie Stew with Cheesy
    Breadsticks

JEFFREY IRVINE
Whole Wheat, Flaxseed,
    and Blueberry Pancakes
Sesame Bok Choy
Coconut Milk Rice

KATE JACOBY
Smoked Chile and Tomato
    Quinoa
Korean Grilled Tofu
    "Steak"

WILLOW JAROSH
Ginger-Spiked Peach Fizz
Cardamom-Ginger Chai Tea
Chili-Lime Kale Chips
Cilantro-Pear Vinaigrette
Creamy Green Dip
Steel-Cut Oatmeal Raisin
    Cookies

DAVID JOACHIM
Vegetarian Souvlaki with
    Pita Wraps
Black and White Bean Soup

HEATHER K. JONES
Veggie "Meat" Loaf

Greens and Couscous
Salad

SCOTT JUREK
Roasted Sweet
Potato Wedges

MATTHEW KADEY
PB & Homemade Jelly
Toast
Pesto Egg Cups
Mango Tango Smoothie
Bowl
Cranberry Beet Smoothie
Sweet Potato Puree
Smoothie
Crunchy Curry Peas
Curry Egg Salad Sandwich
Cocoa Black Bean Tacos
Smoky Squash Flatbread
with Balsamic Glaze
Smoky Black Bean Grilled
Cheese
Apple Cheddar Grilled
Cheese
Avocado Basil Soup
Thai Carrot Soup
Quinoa Fruit Salad with
Maple Dressing
Lime-Sesame Dressing
Red Velvet Brownies
Teff-Chocolate Pudding
Banana Chocolate Tacos

DEENA KASTOR
Grilled Vegetable Polenta
Casserole
Avocado Enchiladas

ELYSE KOPECKY
Coconut Curry Lentil Soup
Kale Farro Salad with
Lemon-Miso Dressing

JENNIFER KUSHNIER
Chickpea Tabbouleh Salad

RICH LANDAU
Smoked Chile and Tomato
Quinoa
Korean Grilled Tofu "Steak"

SUE LESCHINE
Chocolate Tofu Pie

MATT LLANO
Green Chile Guacamole
Chipotle–Sweet Potato
Hummus
Veggie Curry Stew
Dark Chocolate Almond
Butter Date Truffles with
Sea Salt

CARYL MAYER
Zucchini Bread
Veggie Stew with Cheesy
Breadsticks

RONNI MAYER
Spaghetti Squash with
Veggie Gratin

**RACHEL MELTZER
WARREN**
Honeydew Lime Cooler
Steel-Cut Oatmeal Raisin
Cookies

JESSICA MIGALA
Chickpea Pesto Tomato
Soup
Red Lentil and Black Bean
Stew
Sweet and Salty Pistachio
Butter

CHRIS MOSIER
Quinoa and Red Lentil
Kitchari
Classic Winter Kale Salad

ADNAN NASIR
Spinach, Berry, and Goat
Cheese Salad

JACQUELINE NEWGENT
Creamy Veggie Dip

**KEN ORINGER,
SAMUEL ADAMS
BREWERY**
Chocolate Bock Carrots

ELLEN PARODI
Veggie English Muffin
Pizza

JEN PATTAP
Chocolate Avocado
Mousse

LORI POWELL
Zucchini Coins
Squash Mashed Potatoes

MEGAN POWERS
Slow-Cooker Apple-
Cinnamon Oatmeal

**KHALIL HYMORE
QUASHA**
PB&J Smoothie

BARBARA QUINN
South-of-the-Border Snack
Mix

DERI REED
Grilled Eggplant Parmesan

PHILLIP RHODES
Whole Wheat Pasta with
Walnuts, Spinach, and
Mozzarella

MICAH RISK
Berry Tasty Smoothie Bowl
Collard Spring Rolls with
Peanut Dipping Sauce
Raw Cardamom-Spiced
Fruit Crisp

RODALE TEST KITCHEN
Fresh Fruit Scones
"Baked" Granola Apples
Green Smoothie
Passion Fruit, Pineapple,
and Mint Cooler
Potato Latkes
Carrot-Parsnip Latkes
Caramelized Shallots
Apple-Pear Sauce
Pumpkin Curry with
Cucumber Raita
Baked Black Bean Rotini
Lentil Spaghetti with
Creamy Porcini Sauce

MIRIAM RUDIN
Grilled Eggplant Parmesan

SHARON SANDERS
Grilled Eggplant Parmesan

DAVID SANTNER
Coconut-Almond Energy
Bars

JOANNA SAYAGO GOLUB
Chocolate Chip Trail Mix
Balls
Roasted Curry Cauliflower
Tofu Peanut Stir-Fry
Spicy Black Bean Burgers
Watermelon, Ginger, and
Cucumber Salad

ALYSSA SHAFFER
Watercress and Radicchio
Salad with Mustard
Vinaigrette

MICHELE STANTEN
Pumpkin Pie Trail Mix
Popcorn

LIZ VACCARIELLO
Breakfast Tacos
Roasted Tomatoes Stuffed
with Quinoa and Herbs
Cuban Rice and Beans

**JULIA
VANTINE-REICHARDT**
Pumpkin Pie Trail Mix
Popcorn

**LAUREL AND REBECCAH
WASSNER**
Coconut-Curry Snack Mix

DEBRA WITT
Postrun Smoothie

**SELENE YEAGER AND THE
EDITORS OF *PREVENTION***
Watermelon Smoothie
Flax Banana Bread

INDEX

ABOUT THE AUTHOR

Heather Mayer Irvine is the former food and nutrition editor for *Runner's World*. She lives and runs in Bethlehem, Pennsylvania, with her husband, Jeff, and their son, Finn. Heather's work has appeared in *Runner's World*, the Associated Press, *Glamour, Discover,* and *HuffPost,* and on Health.com and CNN. She has a marathon best of 3:31, a half-marathon best of 1:34, a 5K-best of 19:46, and 1-mile best of 5:37. Heather has never met a burger or an ice cream sundae she didn't like.